Sunset

ideas for great
bathrooms

By Scott Atkinson and
the Editors of Sunset Books

Menlo Park, California

Sunset Books

VICE PRESIDENT, GENERAL MANAGER: Richard A. Smeby
VICE PRESIDENT, EDITORIAL DIRECTOR: Bob Doyle
PRODUCTION DIRECTOR: Lory Day
DIRECTOR OF OPERATIONS: Rosann Sutherland
MARKETING MANAGER: Linda Barker
ART DIRECTOR: Vasken Guiragossian
SPECIAL SALES: Brad Moses

Staff for This Book

DEVELOPMENTAL EDITOR: Linda J. Selden
COPY EDITOR/INDEXER: Phyllis Elving
PHOTO DIRECTOR/STYLIST: JoAnn Masaoka Van Atta
ART DIRECTOR: Susanne Weihl
ILLUSTRATOR: Beverley Bozarth Colgan
PRINCIPAL PHOTOGRAPHER: Jamie Hadley
PAGE PRODUCTION: Linda M. Bouchard
PREPRESS COORDINATOR: Danielle Javier
PROOFREADER: Mary Roybal

10 9 8 7 6 5 4 3 2 1
First printing June 2005
Copyright©2005, Sunset Publishing
Corporation, Menlo Park, CA 94025.
Third edition. All rights reserved,
including the right of reproduction in
whole or in part in any form.

ISBN 0-376-01331-1
Library of Congress Control
Number: 2004098081
Printed in the United States of America.

For additional copies of *Ideas for Great Bathrooms* or
any other Sunset book, call 1-800-526-5111 or visit us
at www.sunset.com.

Cover main image: Siemasko + Verbridge, architects;
photography by Brian Vanden Brink.
Top left: photography by Paul Whicheloe.
Top middle: photography Courtesy of Kohler.
Top right: photography by John Granen.
Cover design by Vasken Guiragossian.

Contents

Bathrooms Go Public

It may be one of the last private retreats left to any of us, but today's bathroom is definitely in the public eye, design-wise. Bathrooms have become more stylish, more comfortable, and more efficient than ever before—and to reflect the attention they are earning, Sunset makes a splash with this freshly updated and redesigned entry in its "Ideas for Great..." series. Hundreds of photos team with a solid planning primer and scores of shopping tips for bathroom fixtures and materials. Read the book straight through as a detailed planning resource, or simply browse for images and ideas to help your architect or designer understand more clearly what you want.

A large cast of homeowners and bath professionals helped us shape this new edition. We'd especially like to thank Jeff Burton of Bath and Beyond in San Francisco, California, where we photographed many of the latest bath products.

For the names of designers and architects whose work is featured in this book, or for product sources, turn to pages 126–127.

Take the PLUNGE

THESE DAYS, PEOPLE WANT BATHROOMS to be bold, beautiful, and—especially—comfortable. New bathrooms tend to be bigger (although small, jazzy powder rooms abound, too). They tend to be compartmentalized for multiple uses. Many master baths revolve around a soothing whirlpool or soaking tub. The "master suite"—a formal integration of bedroom, bath, and auxiliary spaces—is perhaps the crowning expression of the bathroom's expanded identity. As with today's kitchen design, there's a freer mixing of bathroom materials and styles, an emphasis on lighting, an interest in fine detailing, and a new creativity in cabinetry.

Style, comfort, and efficiency come in many forms, and you'll see hundreds of options in the first section of this book, "Ideas and Inspiration." When it's time to get down to business, turn to the second section, "How to Do It." Ready to start dreaming and scheming? Just turn the page.

Ideas and INSPIRATION

FIRST, LET'S TAKE A TOUR—one designed to show you as many bathrooms as possible. We begin our trip with an overview of bathroom looks and layouts, from tiny powder rooms to luxurious master suites. Next we survey styles, then zero in on fixtures and finishing touches. Along the way, we offer up shopping tips for classic components such as sinks, tubs, tiles, cabinets, and even towel bars. They say a picture's worth a thousand words—so let's get started.

Great *Spaces*

NO LONGER BOUND to the ho-hum 5-by-7 rectangle of the past, today's bathrooms come in all shapes and sizes, from tiny powder rooms to multilevel master suites. To kick-start your planning for a new bath, first define both your available space and your needs. Then take some time to ponder your layout options—you may have more of them than you think!

To aid in the process, we offer a photographic tour. We'll start with small spaces—powder rooms, guest baths, family baths, and children's baths. Along the way, you'll see both classic and novel solutions for space-challenged layouts. We'll also show you some great designs for universal, barrier-free baths that don't *look* barrier-free.

Then we move on to master baths and master suites. These personalized retreats from the workaday world offer amenities like whirlpool tubs, walk-in showers, multiple sinks, striking materials, and dramatic, flexible lighting. The popular master suite is simply any large space that folds bathroom, bedroom, and dressing room into one integrated layout. Satellite areas might house an exercise area, a breakfast bar, a home office, or the latest in home-theater components.

Left: A bath for two adults sports side-by-side glass vessel sinks atop a wall-hung vanity; twin mirrors are wrapped with shimmering glass tile.

Some of the projects featured in the following pages were make-overs of existing rooms, while others borrowed some space from adjoining rooms or pushed out into gardens or side yards. A few are completely new additions or part of new homes built from scratch.

Whatever your space, ask yourself some basic questions. Do you see your new bathroom as strictly functional or as a stylish retreat, outfitted with the latest amenities? Do you want furnishings to be built in or freestanding? Do you want one open area or, if space allows, separate compartments for different uses?

Both open and closed floor plans are depicted in our photo tour. Note the way light, decor, and traffic patterns carry over from one area to another. Think about the indoor-outdoor link: would you like to have a tree-lined view or a pocket garden just outside your bath, or perhaps an outdoor shower or a deck and spa adjacent to the bathroom proper?

Top right: Corners can be a problem, but the sunny, sweeping views from these steel windows make this one a virtue. Cabinets and bench are both crafted from striking salvaged Douglas fir.

Bottom right: It's an open-and-shut case. This flexible, multiroom suite has a sliding wall panel that links a stone-tiled soaking tub with the bedroom beyond.

A cheery, monochromatic color scheme expands a small space. It begins with the 1-inch shower tiles and the birch plywood cabinetry—sealed with amber marine varnish. Even the exposed studs atop one wall have a yellow tone.

Left: Long and slim, a triangular counter eases traffic congestion in a powder room and adds some bonus surface above the toilet.

Above: A subtle curve in both vanity and countertop saves space and echoes the shape of the sink that rises above the counter.

Left: Here's a space-saving trick. Recess the sink—in this case, an antique marble pedestal—inside its own alcove. An arched window in back further stretches the apparent space.

Left: A guest bath can warrant some special materials. This room features textured tiles, a hewn-stone countertop with a copper vessel sink, and mirror-mounted sconces.

Above: Here's a second view of the bath at left, from inside the shower. An acrylic panel with integral decorative reeds passes light both ways through an otherwise dark wall.

Left: Cramped for space? Put an attic to work for you. This platform tub is tucked into the eave's angle; a tubside dormer adds light and a crow's-nest view.

Facing page: In small baths, think small—like this sink with scaled-down vanity cabinet and space-stretching mirror surrounded by tiny mosaic tiles. Open glass shelves, not boxy cabinets, break up the toilet alcove divider.

Below: Kids' baths can be trendy, too. Here, handmade tiles wrap floor, walls, and tub; the concrete counter is great-looking and practically indestructible as well. Note the trim, stylish wall unit.

Left: Mosaic tiles are easy to clean, and their tiny grout spaces are slip resistant. Mosaics also supply a rainbow of color options. Just add some toys to round out the fun.

Above: Paint is an easy way to liven things up. Accent a single drawer in a run, or paint each one a different color. A colorful tile backsplash and even the drawer pulls add energy in this children's bath. The decorative tiles were made by the kids.

Left: This long trough sink provides ample space for two siblings to wash hands or brush teeth at the same time. A pullout bench puts the faucet within reach.

Facing page: This universal shower works hard and still looks great. Wrapped in marble tiles, it includes user-friendly features such as a padded curb, a padded bench, brass grab bars, and an adjustable-height hand shower.

Right: A barrier-free wall sink, an angled mirror, and a cantilevered counter are easily approachable bathroom amenities. The tub's grab bars and sinkside shower controls are handy and handsome.

Above: A cantilevered concrete sink allows access for a wheelchair. The drainpipes are wrapped with coils of tubing to prevent contact with hot pipes.

Right: This barrier-free master bath includes floor-level duckboards for easy wheelchair access and good drainage, plus a long bathing bench that provides a seat near the hand shower and facilitates getting in and out of the tub.

Below: Inside meets outside in this owner-built master-suite bath featuring meticulous tilework, glass block, and a French door that opens to the nearby private garden and in-ground spa pool.

Above: A stainless-steel spa fronts a private pocket courtyard. Sliding steel doors can be pulled back when the weather warrants.

Left: This outdoor shower is accessed from a master bath's dressing area—the only way to accommodate a decent-size bedroom and bathroom. Fears of cold and lack of privacy were quickly dispatched by the spa-like feel.

Below: Here's a look at one wing of a master bath (also shown in the bottom photo), including one user's sink, cabinets, and open shelves. The walk-in shower is seen to the left.

Left: A couple's symmetrical master bath centers on the freestanding tub. Each user has a personal space on a flanking wall (see top photo).

Above: This master suite offers beautifully matched marble, a spacious walk-in shower with multiple heads and jets, a makeup center, a second sink area (not visible in photo), and a walk-in dressing room.

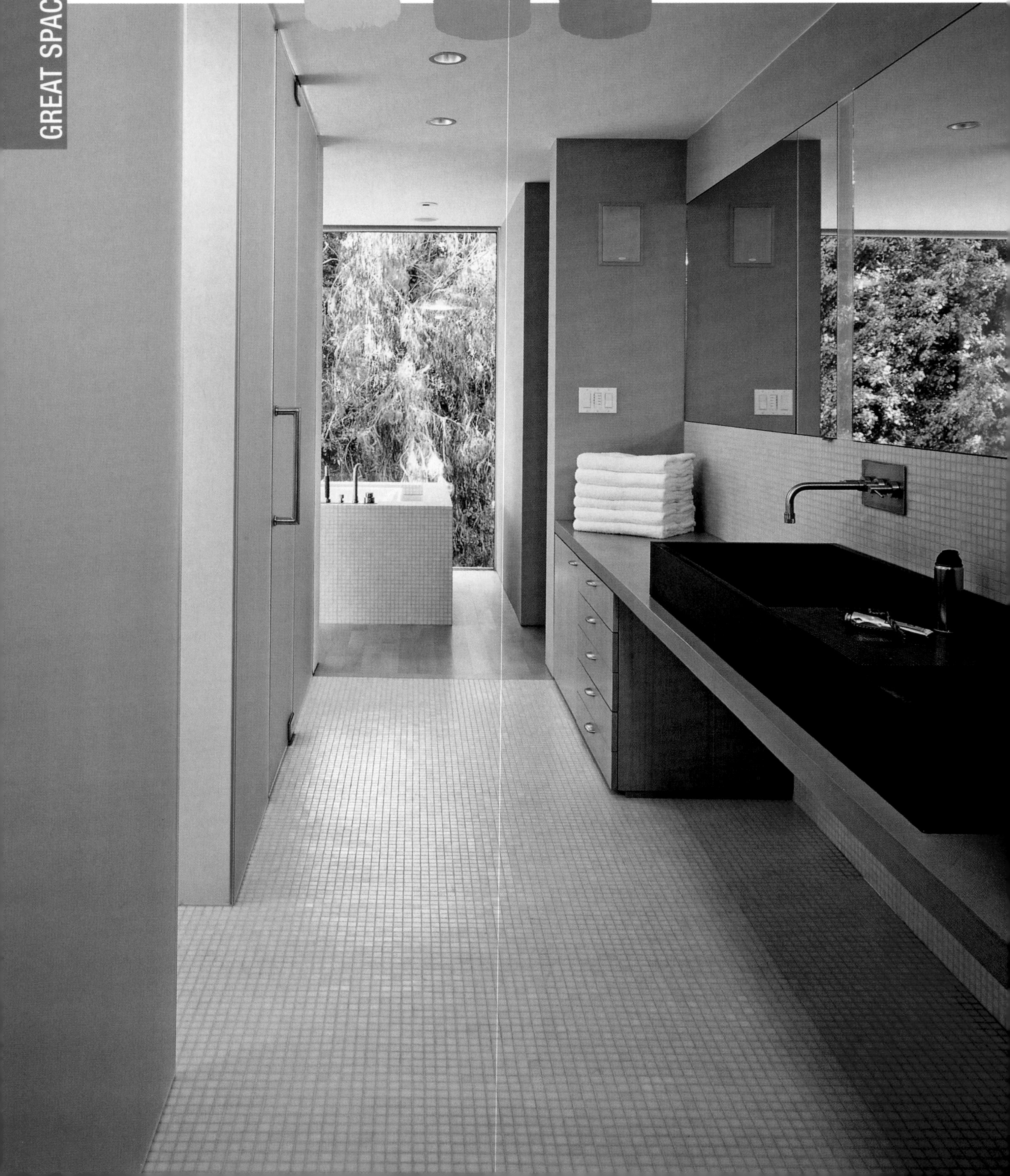

Facing page: A corridor-style, open-plan suite features a custom granite sink, oak counter and cabinets, mosaic floor tiles with beech flooring beyond, a pedestal spa to the rear, and separate shower and toilet compartments.

Above: The adjacent dressing area has banks of built-in, floor-to-ceiling cabinets and a vertical view of the woods outside.

Right: Here's a look across the pedestal spa through to the bath proper and down to the linked bedroom beyond.

What's
Your Style?

NOW IT'S TIME to start thinking about your bathroom's decor. On the following pages, we've brought together many different looks and colors. Style is highly personal, so of course you won't be drawn to all of these, but which ones *will* you like? Your reactions, even the negative ones, can start you in the right direction. You might want to show your favorites to your design professional.

First off, do you want things streamlined or unfitted? High-tech or homey? The two main poles of bathroom style are traditional and contemporary. Included in the style spectrum are period, regional, country, romantic, global, and eclectic looks—to name a few. Hybrids abound. Many designs strive to blend traditional looks with modern amenities such as whirlpool baths and steam showers.

Style is cumulative: it's built up from fixtures, furnishings, surfaces, color combinations, window styles, light fixtures, even cabinet pulls. Sound complicated? It's not, really. If your home's architecture has a distinctive style, take a cue from that. On the other hand, many modern homes provide a neutral backdrop. Wallpaper, a whirlpool, an antique sink, or some wall sconces can serve as a starting point, and the bathroom design grows from there. Eclectic looks and some country decors

Left: Shaker simple, this timeless bath also folds in the latest options, including a porcelain vessel sink, a long-necked wall spout, and elegant mirrorside sconces.

intentionally mix and match disparate elements into one-of-a-kind styles.

Moods are established, at least in part, by the materials you choose for countertops, floor coverings, and wall and ceiling treatments. Besides time-tested tile, vinyl, and laminate, we're seeing more stone in baths—the result of newly affordable stone-tile offerings and the sealers that protect them. Glass mosaic tiles are hot news, too. Other popular materials include hand-painted art tiles, terrazzo, plaster, solid-surface composites, textiles, and glass block. Wood and carpeting are also showing up on floors, especially in detached areas away from direct-splash zones.

Beyond aesthetic considerations, you will want to weigh the physical characteristics of surface materials. Most bathrooms take a lot of wear. Is your countertop choice water resistant, durable, and easy to maintain? Is the floor uncomfortable to walk on, noisy, or slippery? Are walls easy to clean? A powder room or master suite might be the place to try delicate materials that would be impractical in a family bathroom.

Top right: Clean white woodwork, hand-painted tile, and pretty pink wallpaper distinguish this fastidiously detailed, romantic-style bath.

Bottom right: Bright, brash tiles completely coat all available surfaces in this bath, even the customized console sink.

Dressed in glass and stone tiles, a contemporary bath features rectangles of various sizes, punctuated by the floating black vanity and its twin vessel sinks atop a limestone counter.

Left: This design in a tall, skinny space illustrates what you might call luxurious minimalism, with industrial-looking plumbing fixtures and fittings providing their own sense of repose.

Above: As distinctive as sculpture, or modern furniture, this spare and stylish vanity glows in the light spilling from a slit window beyond.

Left: This tiny bath is the only one in the house, so every inch counts. A space-saving counter directs the traffic flow and leads the eye to the tiled pedestal tub.

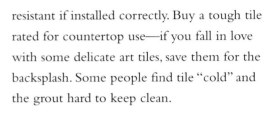

Comparing *Countertops*

MARBLE

Plastic laminate, ceramic tile, solid-surface acrylic, and stone are the four major countertop materials in current favor for bathrooms.

Durable and economical, laminate is available in a multitude of colors, textures, and patterns. Ready-made counters are called "post-formed"; custom-fabricated countertops offer far more choices and edge treatments. On the downside, laminate can scratch, chip, and stain; high-gloss laminates show every smudge. Postformed tops are inexpensive, but they can also *look* cheap.

Stylish ceramic tile comes in many colors, textures, and patterns, and it is heat and water resistant if installed correctly. Buy a tough tile rated for countertop use—if you fall in love with some delicate art tiles, save them for the backsplash. Some people find tile "cold" and the grout hard to keep clean.

Solid-surface tops are durable, water resistant, and easy to clean—this marblelike material can be shaped and joined with nearly invisible seams. However, it's expensive, requiring professional fabrication and installation for best results.

Granite, marble, and limestone are beautiful, natural stone materials. Stone is water resistant, heatproof, and extremely durable. Oil, alcohol, and any acid can stain marble or limestone, but granite stands up to all of these. Solid slabs are very expensive. Stone tiles—including slate—are a less costly alternative.

PLASTIC LAMINATE

SOLID-SURFACE ACRYLIC

Synthetic marble, while still a common countertop choice available at home centers, is losing some ground to solid-surface materials. Custom glass, stainless steel, and cast concrete are gaining in popularity, especially in high-style master suites and powder rooms. Wood is sometimes used for countertops; to prevent water damage, wood counters must be treated (perhaps repeatedly) with a durable finish.

CERAMIC TILE

CONCRETE WITH
RECYCLED GLASS

LIMESTONE

GRANITE

Right: It's a classic, from the traditional pedestal sink to white frame-and-panel cabinets, hardwood floors, candelabra wall sconces, and a butterfly collection in wood frames.

Below: Tumbled marble tiles lead the way to a formal pedestal tub. Clear-finished natural wood and a decorative ceiling pendant complete the picture.

Above: The spa travels west. A Japanese-inspired master bath features an insulated stainless-steel soaking tub, flagstone flooring with cozy radiant heat, hanging hemlock cabinets, cantilevered walnut bench, twin integral sinks, and plenty of open space. Celadon-colored plaster provides a soothing backdrop.

Left: Fabric-lined framed panels, a porcelain console sink and marble counter, traditional wall sconces, and an oval mirror paint a fine formal picture.

Flooring *Facts*

"FLOATING" WOOD PLANKS

The primary requirements for a bathroom floor are moisture resistance and durability. Resilient tiles and sheets, ceramic tiles, and properly sealed masonry or hardwood are all good candidates.

Most commonly made from solid vinyl or polyurethane, resilient flooring is flexible, moisture and stain resistant, easy to install, and simple to maintain. Tiles can be mixed to form custom patterns or provide color accents. Sheets run up to 12 feet wide, eliminating the need to seam in many bathrooms. Prices are generally modest, but expect to pay a premium for custom tiles and imported products.

Ceramic tiles are usually classified as quarry tiles, commonly tough, unglazed red-clay tiles; terra-

cotta, unglazed tiles in earth tones; porcelain pavers, rugged tiles in stonelike shades and textures; and glazed floor tiles, available in glossy, matte, or textured finish. Costs range from inexpensive to moderate; porcelain is the priciest.

Natural stone such as slate, marble, granite, and limestone has been used for flooring for centuries. Pieces generally are butted tightly together; irregular flagstones require wider grout joints. The cost of masonry can be quite high, and certain stones—including marble and limestone—absorb stains and dirt readily. Careful sealing is essential.

For safety's sake, a bathroom floor must be slip resistant, especially in wet areas. Tiles, either ceramic or stone, are safest in a matte or textured finish. Smaller ceramic tiles, with the increased number of grout surfaces they require, offer extra traction.

PORCELAIN PAVERS

SLATE

CARPET

TERRAZZO

Don't be afraid to mix and match flooring materials. Today's layouts often use different materials to define wet and dry areas. Cozy carpeting, especially the newer stain-resistant type, is showing up in dressing areas, grooming centers, and even exercise rooms. Hardwood strips or planks can play a similar role in period or country designs. "Floating" floor systems have several veneered strips atop each backing board, and you'll now find "planks" and "tiles" of high-pressure laminate that look surprisingly like the real thing—just be sure your warranty covers bathroom use.

LAMINATE TILES

VINYL SHEET

TILE MOSAIC

Below: Surrounded by warm wood, this country
bathroom's freestanding tub calls out for a long, lazy soak.

Above: Country motifs abound here, including beaded wall paneling and tub skirt, wood-frame windows, and floor diamonds painted on wide pine boards.

Left: The "recipe" here calls for separate found object—an antique wall-hung sink, a folk-art mirror, and a bright blue recycled chest.

Facing page: Don't be afraid to mix and match styles, colors, and textures. This view joins terra-cotta with colorful accent tiles, plastered walls, hand-hewn wood mirror frames, and striking Italianesque wall sconces—plus a pop of paint color in the built-in shelf unit.

Right: An artful, homeowner-designed tile seascape flows in and out of a walk-in shower.

Above: Blending unexpected materials is not a crime. Galvanized steel roofing moves from the barn to this bath, joining cottage-style beadboard and hardwood flooring.

Right: A retro design combines plywood, marble, fiberglass roofing panels, and green mosaic tiles.

What about *Walls?*

LATEX PAINT

Along with the shower and tub-surround areas, your bathroom will probably include a good bit of wall space. All these surfaces must be able to withstand moisture, heat, and high usage. Your wall treatments will also go a long way toward defining the look of your room.

Paint

Everybody thinks of paint first. But what kind is best for the bathroom? Latex is easy to work with, and you can clean up wet paint easily with soap and water. Alkyd paint (often called oil-base) provides high gloss and will hang on a little harder than latex, but it's trickier to apply, emits more fumes, and requires cleanup with mineral spirits. Whichever you choose, the higher the resin content, the tougher and glossier the paint usually is; look for products labeled gloss, semigloss, or satin if you want a durable, washable finish.

Tile

Ceramic wall tiles, typically glazed, offer great variety in color and design. Made by machine, these thin, light tiles have precise shapes—they're usually set close together, with narrow ($\frac{1}{16}$-inch) grout lines. Common sizes include 3-inch, $4\frac{1}{4}$-inch, and 6-inch squares; larger squares and rectangles may also be available.

GLASS TILES

Decorative art tiles make striking accents in a field of less expensive wall tiles, especially in low-impact areas such as backsplashes and tub surrounds. Tiny mosaic tiles—both ceramic and glass—are popular these days; they come premounted on mesh backings, so you don't need to set and straighten them one by one.

New diamond-saw techniques have made stone tiles, once a luxury, competitive in price with quality ceramic products. Popular offerings include marble, granite, limestone, and slate; less common are onyx, travertine, and quartzite. Polished stone is traditional, but rougher texturing like honing and tumbling are gaining prominence—both for easier maintenance and for the matte, pastel looks they produce. Stone mosaic panels come premounted on mesh backings.

TUMBLED MARBLE

Wallpaper

The ideal bathroom wallpaper is
scrubbable, durable, and stain resistant.
Vinyl wallpaper, in a wide variety of
colors and textures, fills the bill. New
patterns, some of which replicate
other surfaces (such as linen), tend to
be subtle. A wallpaper border adds
visual punch to ceiling lines and wall
openings.

Textile wall coverings come in many
colors and textures, casual to formal.
Keep in mind that most textiles fray
easily, can't be washed (though most
accept a spray-on stain repellent), and
are subject to damage from bathroom
moisture; it's often best to save them
for powder rooms, guest baths, or dry
areas in master suites.

Wood

Solid wood paneling—natural,
stained, bleached, or painted—adds
a warm feel to formal and country
decor schemes. Wainscoting is traditional, with a chair rail separating
wood paneling below from the
painted or papered wall above.

Generally, solid boards have edges
specially milled to overlap or
interlock.

Moldings are back in vogue. You'll
find basic profiles at lumberyards and
home centers, while specialty mill-
work shops are likely to have a wider
selection and often can custom-
match an old favorite for you.

WALLPAPER

WOOD WAINSCOTING

Water
Workings

YOUR CHOICES OF SINK, TUB, AND/OR SHOWER—
and the fittings that go with them—will do a lot to determine how
your bathroom is used, how its traffic flows, and what kind of general
ambience it has. On the following pages, we put the spotlight on these
often unsung heroes of style and function. For a closer look at fixture
layouts and clearances, see pages 96–103 of the "How to Do It" section.

No longer just a basin and a mirror, the sink
area has become an orchestrated environment
for personal care. Layouts with two sinks—in
one continuous vanity, in side-by-side alcoves,
or on opposite walls—are popular. Some bathrooms include a separate, smaller washbasin in
the toilet compartment or makeup area.

Sinks and faucets have become design
accents in their own right—a relatively low-
commitment way to add a bit of dash to an
otherwise restrained design scheme. (If you
later decide you don't like the boldness, it's a
lot simpler to change a faucet than a shower
or tub surround.) Deck-mounted and integral
sinks are sporting new looks, and you'll see
pedestal and wall-hung sinks in a rainbow of
colors and finishes and in classic, retro, and
contemporary styles. Or how about a sculptural above-counter basin? Faucets and
fittings likewise come in all sorts of new
shapes and finishes.

Left: A powder room provides a great opportunity for
some extra pizzazz. This translucent wall sink plays off
the glass tile and colored stone backing it.

Tubs form another focal point—a symbol of luxury and repose. You can choose a basic bathtub or a classic, freestanding clawfoot or slipper model. Pedestal tubs present a seamless, built-in look. Whirlpool tubs with many jet options abound. Or consider a traditional soaking tub in acrylic, wood, or tile.

Tub/shower units save space, but most users prefer to have a separate shower if there's room. Though market offerings include a plethora of prefabricated stalls, it's worth taking a look at the larger, custom walk-in shower—perhaps with a built-in bench. A well-designed shower is also safer to use than many tub/showers, which may lack firm footing and adequate grab bars. Frameless glass walk-ins are trendy; or take it even further with a doorless, curbless shower "room." Showers are even moving outdoors.

Shower heads and jets are the new big thing; they come in both multiple and adjustable versions, with preset temperature controls and scaldproof mixing valves.

Top right: A casual, open shower has minimalist controls (actually shutoff valves) and meets the outdoors via a swinging, light-diffusing privacy panel.

Bottom right: Bubbling and steaming, this sturdy wooden soaking tub can be screened from the bedroom by means of a sliding shoji-inspired panel. A peeled tree trunk houses shower head and plumbing.

Below: Wood can hold water, too, as demonstrated by this graceful bentwood trough with glass dam in front. A built-in shelf holds votive candles and hides the faucet workings.

Above: The symmetry of twin console sinks with twin mirrors and flanking wall sconces is fitting for a formal decor.

Left: Try to find the faucet downspout—it's tucked below the raised section of the stainless-steel counter behind the integral sink. Only the minimalist faucet handles are visible.

Above: A deck-mounted sink *is* the deck—in this case, perched atop a spare, tapered vanity base.

Far left: A crystal vessel sink rises above a transparent shelf in a small powder room. Drain fittings run through the glass countertop, making a design statement of their own.

Near left: Pressed for space? Install a shallow cabinet run, then hang a cantilevered Euro-style sink off the front edge.

Sinks
and Faucets

HAND-PAINTED
SINK

SINGLE-LEVER
FAUCET

Bathroom sinks are big news. Stroll through most any showroom and you'll see a huge array of styles, shapes, and colors. Here are your basic options.

Deck-mounted sinks

The vanity-bound basin is still the most common setup. You'll find deck mounts in a wide selection of materials, including vitreous china, fiberglass-reinforced plastic, enameled steel, and enameled cast iron. Cost runs the gamut from moderate to quite expensive.

Other possible materials include translucent glass, hand-painted ceramic, stainless steel, brass, copper, and even wood. These may be strikingly elegant as accents but can require zealous maintenance.

Deck-mounted models may offer a choice of mounting methods. Self-rimming sinks with molded overlaps, supported by the edge of the countertop cutout, are the easiest to install. Flush sinks have surrounding metal strips to hold the basin to the countertop; unrimmed sinks are recessed below the countertop. Vessel sinks, designed as seemingly "freestanding" sculptural basins, sit atop the counter and drain down through it.

Integral sinks

A countertop with an integral bowl has no joints, so installation and cleaning are easy. Sink color can match or complement the countertop; for example, you might choose a cream-colored sink below a granite-patterned counter. Edge-banding and other border options abound.

VESSEL SINK

PEDESTAL SINK

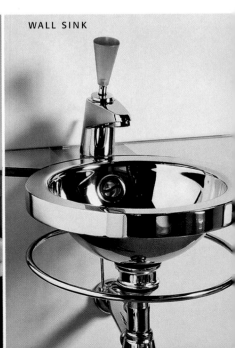

WALL SINK

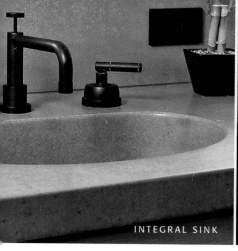

INTEGRAL SINK

SPREAD-FIT FAUCET

VESSEL FAUCET

Solid-surface offerings (page 28) are numerous. Other integral sinks come in cast polymers (such as cultured marble), vitreous china, and fiberglass. Most are custom orders, though most home centers stock cultured-marble versions.

Pedestal, wall, and console sinks

Pedestal sinks are making a big comeback, in a wide range of both traditional and modern designs. Typically made of vitreous china, these elegant towers consist of two parts: the bowl and the column, or pedestal. The pedestal often, but not always, hides the plumbing (though pipes can be tricky to hook up). Some pedestal sinks can be adjusted for height.

Like pedestals, wall sinks are enjoying new popularity. Materials and styles are along the same lines as for pedestals; some designs come in both versions. Generally speaking, wall-hung models are among the least expensive and most compact sinks.

If you like the look of pedestal or wall sinks but yearn for a bit more elbow room, take a look at console sinks. These "stretch models" join a wider rectangular deck with either two or four furniture-like vanity legs. Some include open storage space below.

Faucets

The world of sink faucets, like that of sinks themselves, is constantly expanding to offer new colors, shapes, styles, and accessories. There are faucets with digital temperature readout or scaldproof workings, or both, and spouts that automatically stop the flow when you remove your hand. How about a swiveling European faucet with adjustable spray, drinking spout, and gum-massage attachment?

SINGLE-LEVER FAUCET

Sink faucets are available with single, center-set, or spread-fit controls. A single-lever fitting has a combined faucet and lever or knob controlling water flow and temperature. A center-set control has separate hot and cold water controls and faucet mounted on a base or escutcheon. A spread-fit control has detached hot and cold controls and an independently mounted faucet.

Whatever style you choose, professionals agree that you get what you pay for. Solid-brass workings, though pricey, are considered the most durable. Ceramic-disk and plastic-disk designs generally are easier to maintain than washer schemes.

WALL FAUCET

CENTER-SET FAUCET

45

Left: A stainless-steel soaking tub occupies a corner below windows that have partially sandblasted glass panels. The nearby surfaces are clad with marble and slate tiles and plaster tinted a terra-cotta color.

Facing page: A freestanding clawfoot tub is the perfect centerpiece for a romantic decor scheme.

Below: A traditional Japanese soaking tub has pride of place in this tile-lined bathroom. An open shower is just a few steps beyond.

ACRYLIC WHIRLPOOL TUBS

Tubs
and Fittings

TUB SPOUT DIVERTER

The market overflows with bathtub styles. No longer does the 30- by 60-inch tub, designed to fit the dimensions of the standard 5- by 7-foot bathroom of the past, rule your choice.

The basic built-in

Standard tubs come in two basic configurations: recessed and corner. Recessed tubs fit an alcove between two side walls and a back wall; they have a finished front "apron" and come with drain openings on either the left or right side. Corner models have one side and one end finished. Some stylish tubs are finished on three sides, allowing placement along an open wall.

The boxy standard tub is enameled steel, relatively inexpensive, and lightweight—but noisy, cold, and prone to chipping. Built-to-last enameled cast-iron tubs are more durable and warmer to the touch, but they are very heavy and may require structural reinforcement.

These days, the most innovative tubs tend to be plastic—either vacuum-formed acrylic or injection-molded fiberglass. Plastic tubs are usually designed for platform or sunken installation. The one drawback: dark, colorful fiberglass surfaces tend to scratch or dull easily.

So-called soaking tubs have deep interiors. They come in recessed, platform, and corner models, with rectangular or round interiors of fiberglass or acrylic.

Freestanding tubs

An old-fashioned freestanding model like the enduring clawfoot tub makes a nice focal point in a traditional or country decor. You can buy either a new reproduction or a reconditioned original. Freestanding slipper tubs have an extended back for comfortable lounging.

Whirlpool tubs

Think of these hydromassage units simply as deep bathtubs with jets. Most models resemble standard acrylic platform tubs; a pump and venturi jets create the whirlpool effect.

SLIPPER TUB

ANTIQUE HANDSET

DECK-MOUNTED FITTINGS

Jet designs vary—you can opt for high pressure and low volume (a few strong jets) or low pressure and high volume (lots of softer jets). Some new models feature blower-driven air jets, which are easier to maintain. You'll even find air jets in clawfoot or slipper tubs.

Want extras? Consider adding a digital temperature control, a timer, a built-in fill spout, or a cushy neck roll. Some models allow the pump to be installed in a remote location, making for a quieter soak.

Tub fittings

For combination tub/shower units, you can opt for single or separate controls. Tubs require a spout and a drain; tub/showers need a spout, a shower head (see page 53), a diverter valve, and a drain. The best fittings have solid brass workings. Many finishes are offered, including chrome, brass, nickel, pewter, gold plate, and enameled epoxy. You'll also find color-coordinated pop-up drains and overflow plates.

Roman or waterfall spouts look striking and can fill tubs much faster than standard fittings—assuming your supply pipes (see page 118) are up to the task.

Unfortunately, tubs (especially whirlpools) aren't the best option for really getting clean. For that, add a separate hand shower controlled by a nearby diverter valve.

SOAKING TUB

ROMAN TUB SPOUT

49

Right: A curbless walk-in shower has an open feel but is screened by a floor-to-ceiling panel of frosted glass.

Below: A walk-in, sealed steam shower is the focal point of a master suite splashed with intensely green Venetian-glass tile.

Call it the wet blue room. Integrally colored plaster walls, a concrete counter, and a gray concrete floor with a central drain create a distinctive open showering sanctuary.

Far left: It's okay to have fun with tile! This funky handcrafted shower mosaic was fashioned from broken tile chips.

Near left: Floating atop an interior rock garden, a shower lined with corrugated steel lets bathers enjoy the view through a clear glass wall.

Shower *Styles*

SHOWER PANS

COORDINATED FITTINGS

Select a prefabricated shower stall, match separate manufactured components, or build your shower completely from scratch. Whichever way you choose to go, think about shower heads and controls. Also consider amenities such as a comfortable bench or fold-down seat, adjustable or handheld shower heads, a place for shampoos and shaving equipment, and sturdy grab bars.

Prefabricated shower stalls

If your remodel calls for moving walls or doors, you may be able to fit a one-piece molded shower or tub/shower surround through the opening—though these units are really designed for new homes or additions. One-piece showers are available in fiberglass-reinforced gelcoat, longer-lasting acrylic, plastic laminate, and synthetic marble. For comfort, choose a shower that is at least 30 inches across on the inside—preferably 36 inches.

The term "shower stall" needn't mean something boxy or boring. Circular, corner, and angular wraparounds are available with enough spray heads and accessories to please the most demanding shower connoisseur. Circular showers often have clear or tinted acrylic doors that double as walls.

Build your own

One way to end up with exactly the shower you want is to mix and match base, surround, and doors.

A shower base or "pan" can be purchased separately or in a kit that includes the shower surround. Most bases are made of fiberglass, terrazzo, cast polymer, or solid-surface materials. It's easy to find a base that works with a tub, since many manufacturers produce both. You can also build a pan from mortar and masonry, but this is a job for a pro.

Shower surrounds require solid framing for support. Choose prefabricated wall panels, or use a custom wall treatment such as ceramic tile, stone, or a solid-surface material over a waterproof backing. Molded wall panels of fiberglass or synthetic marble may include integral soap dishes, ledges, grab bars, and other accessories. These manufactured panels are sized for easy transport, to be assembled and seamed on-site.

Shower doors come in swinging, sliding, folding, and pivoting styles. Doors and enclosures are commonly made of tempered safety glass with aluminum framing. The glazing itself can be clear, hammered, pebbled, tinted, or striped. The frameless or seamless look is popular, though pricey.

SEAMLESS GLASS DOOR

PREFAB CORNER SHOWER

The spray's the thing

"Multiple" and "adjustable" are the bywords for today's shower fittings. Large walk-in showers often have two or more shower heads—fixed heads at different levels and/or hand units on adjustable vertical bars.

"Surround" designs combine one or more fixed heads with wall-mounted auxiliary jets or adjustable multijet vertical bars. You can also buy pre-assembled, columnlike control panels that house all these goodies. How do you adjust all those jets? Diverters may have three or more settings for orchestrating multiple water sources.

Safety plays a part in new designs, too. If you've ever suffered a pressure drop when someone flushes a toilet or starts the washer, you'll appreciate single-control shower fittings with pressure balancing to prevent scalding rises in temperature. Quick-reacting thermostatic valves are also available, with or without digital readouts.

GLASS-BLOCK
WALK-IN SHOWER

SHOWER HEAD
DIVERTER

"SHAMPOO"
SHOWER HEADS

DIVERTER
VALVE WITH
HAND SHOWER

SHOWER
CONTROL
PANEL

Toilets *and Bidets*

PRESSURE-ASSISTED TOILET TANK

ELECTRONIC
TOILET/
BIDET

New styling, new colors, and new efficiency have all but recast the tried-and-true water closet. In addition to standard and antique styles, vitreous china toilets now come in sleek European designs. Do you want classic white, shiny black, or a soft pastel? Ultra-low-flush or pressure-assisted mechanics?

The bidet, a European standby used primarily for personal hygiene, is gaining popularity on this side of the Atlantic. Like toilets, bidets are made of vitreous china, in a range of styles, colors, and finishes to match other fixtures.

Toilets

As water becomes a scarcer resource, the new word in toilets is ultra-low-flush (ULF). Older toilets use 5 to 7 gallons or more per flush, but in 1994 the codes were changed to require 1.6-gallon-per-flush toilets for new construction. Some water districts even offer a rebate if you install a ULF fixture in your present home.

Many homeowners complain that low-flush toilets are really no-flush toilets, requiring several flushings. One response to this problem has been bigger flush valves, more efficient flush mechanisms, better bowl washing, and clog-resistant siphon outlets. Another option is the pressure-assisted design, which uses a strong air vacuum to power a quick, intensive flush. Pressure-assisted models are noisier than other low-flush toilets, but just for a moment.

The basic style choice in toilets is between traditional two-piece and European one-piece designs. A two-piece toilet has a separate tank that's either bolted directly to the bowl or, in the case of some period reproductions, mounted on the wall above. One-piece models are also known as "lowboy" or "low-profile" toilets. Bowls can be round or elongated. Some toilets come with seats and lids, some don't. If you're splurging, you might consider an electronic seat that's heated and/or programmed with a bidet-like spray jet.

Before buying a new toilet for an older house, check the offset—the distance between the back wall and the center of the drain hub (measured to the hold-down nuts). Most newer models are designed for a 12-inch offset.

WALL-MOUNTED
TOILET

Bidets

A bidet, best installed next to the toilet, is floor-mounted and plumbed with hot and cold water and a sink-size (1½-inch) drain. It comes with either a horizontal spray mount or a vertical spray in the center of the bowl. Controls may be deck- or wall-mounted, single or double. Most versions have a pop-up stopper that allows the unit to double as a foot-bath or a laundry basin.

Some bidets drain through a floor outlet and floor trap, like toilets. Most new models, however, have built-in traps and drain through the wall. If you've chosen a vertical-spray version, you'll need a standpipe, or vacuum breaker, to keep any waste water from backing up— that's the vertical brass pipe shown below right.

COMPACT TWO-PIECE TOILET

TRADITIONAL TWO-PIECE TOILET

ONE-PIECE TOILET WITH MATCHING BIDET

VERTICAL-SPRAY BIDET

Bright *Ideas*

A GOOD LIGHTING PLAN provides shadow-free, no-glare illumination for the entire bath as well as bright, uniform light for specific tasks. And as you'll see, both lighting fixtures and openings to let in light can also add striking visual effects. Remember, too, that mirrors, light-toned room colors, and smooth textures all help spread available light around a room.

Natural daylight can enter a bathroom through windows, skylights, doors, or all three. When a bathroom faces the street or the neighbors, it may be best to trade a little light for privacy. Glass block, translucent glazing, and decorative glass—stained, sand-blasted, or beveled—can deliver decorative flair while maintaining a reserved exterior. Interior glazing or block lets light pass from space to space in compartmentalized layouts.

When the sun goes down, you'll need good artificial lighting. The trick is to provide task light that's gently flattering yet strong enough for grooming. Be sure to choose warm-toned bulbs or tubes with good color-rendering properties for accurate makeup lighting and reliable skin tones.

Other use areas—such as tub, shower, and toilet compartments—may need auxiliary lighting. In particular, walk-in showers can

Left: Random, playful colored chinks in a gray-plastered wall let in light and some edited views without sacrificing privacy.

become dark caves. Light fixtures in showers must be sealed units approved for wet locations; some designers are turning to outdoor or even pool fixtures.

Fluorescent sources can give good general lighting, and they are required in some energy-conscious areas. In-direct fixtures work well; consider cove lighting, soffit lighting, trans-lucent diffusers, and other bounce sources that spread soft, even light.

Guest baths, master baths, and especially master suites often call for layered lighting schemes that include accent and/or decorative fixtures. Low-voltage downlights are great for accent and display needs. If you wish to draw attention to the fix-tures themselves, consider decorative pendants, custom wall sconces, or whimsical cable lights.

Multiple sources and multiple controls allow you to alternate between morning efficiency and nighttime repose. Consider dimmers here. Also plan to provide low-energy night lighting for safety and convenience.

Top right: Double casement windows above the pedestal sink swing outward, bringing light, fresh air, and a view of the outside world to the bath. You'll just need to put the mirror somewhere else.

Bottom right: Workaday sinkside porcelain wall sockets retain some of their down-home feel but are dressed up and shielded by "lodge-style" twigs supporting translucent diffusers.

Facing page: During daylight hours, decorative glass is a source of subtle ambient light. At night, stylish wall sconces, discreet downlights, and a playful undercounter glow take over.

Left: Glass block makes a striking, light-refracting shower surround. It's a natural for diffused privacy screens, too.

Above: Ganged steel windows and matching skylights wrap light around a pedestal tub.

Left: Hinged wood-framed windows surround a granite-wrapped pedestal tub, opening the bathroom directly to the deck and landscape beyond. At night, a single pendant shines forth.

Right: A triangular niche with thick glass shelves is lit from behind, highlighting objects while adding an ambient glow to the room.

Above: Doors, too, can pass light to the bath—as long as they maintain privacy. Here, a frosted-glass pocket door teams with an oversize transom. When the bath is not in use, the door stays open.

Right: A shower that's remote from the tubside window shares its light, thanks to a clear glass surround.

Facing page: The window brings in light, the glass block adds more, and clear shower glass—plus reflective white tile—spreads it around the room.

Facing page: A mirror-faced cabinet is broken by flush-mounted incandescent tubes for makeup light, and backsplash and counter areas are washed by additional light from beneath the cabinet. A double-hung window further brightens the room.

Right: A ceiling panel evenly diffuses the light from a bright tungsten fixture above this shower enclosure.

Below: A diffused inset fixture puts makeup light right where it's needed. Additional ambient light glows from a translucent panel housed in the display niche.

Left: Low, wall-recessed lights mark the path from bed to bathroom in a master suite; they can be turned on by themselves for soft fill light or to guide late-night passage.

Above: The fixed lamps for this makeup table have a classic feel and are wired right up through the countertop, leaving no cord clutter.

Left: These twin sinks are lit via fluorescent bars behind and below the glass countertops, bouncing light off both the wall and the cabinet tops.

Facing page: Wall sconces flank the mirror-fronted cabinet, providing warm and welcoming grooming light in a small powder room. The glass-block wall brings extra light from an adjacent room to this windowless space.

DOWNLIGHT
HOUSINGS

Bulbs
and Fixtures

HALOGEN PAR
BULB

Good lighting can make or break your bathroom design. Lighting pros agree: pick the bulbs first, then the fixtures to house them.

Here's a quick rundown of your lighting options. For more about lighting terms and practices, see pages 112–113.

HALOGEN
MR-16

Light bulbs and tubes

Incandescent light, the old standby, is produced by a tungsten thread that burns slowly inside a glass bulb. A-bulbs are the classics; PAR bulbs produce a more controlled beam; silvered-bowl and frosted bulbs diffuse light. Decorative bulbs are also available.

COMPACT
FLUORESCENTS

Unrivaled for energy efficiency, fluorescent tubes produce shadowless light when mercury vapor is burned inside and reradiated by a phosphor coating. They last far longer than incandescent bulbs. In many areas, ambient lighting for new bathrooms must be fluorescent.

While older fluorescent tubes drew criticism for noise, flicker, and poor color rendition, the first two problems have been remedied by electronic ballasts and better fixture shielding. As for color, manufacturers have developed fluorescents in a wide

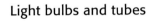

FLUORESCENT
TUBE

spectrum of hues, from very warm (about 2,700°K) to very cool (about 6,300°K) as measured in degrees Kelvin on the color thermometer.

PL-fluorescents look like small traditional tubes bent back on themselves, allowing fluorescent light to be used in smaller, trimmer fixtures—recessed downlights, for instance. Compact fluorescents (CFLs) directly replace incandescent A-bulbs; you simply screw a CFL into a standard fixture socket.

Bright, white quartz halogen sources are excellent for task lighting, pinpoint accenting, and other dramatic effects. They also last far longer than their incandescent rivals. Low-voltage halogen lights are especially useful for accent lighting; operating on 12 or 24 volts, these require transformers, sometimes built in, to step down standard 120-volt household current.

The popular MR-16 halogen creates the tightest beam; for a longer reach and wider coverage, choose a halogen PAR bulb. But be advised: some PAR bulbs, particularly low-voltage ones, can produce a hum, especially when dimmed.

SILVERED-
BOWL BULB

INCANDESCENT BULBS

Fixture types

Recessed downlights and surface-mounted fixtures are the two mainstays of bathroom lighting.

Recessed downlights, in both low- and standard-voltage versions, offer effective light without the intrusion of a visible fixture. Basically domes into which light bulbs are set, most downlights can be fitted with a number of bulb types and sizes, trims, and accessories that shape the light to the desired function. When installed, only the trim is visible, not the fixture itself.

"New-work" downlights, used in new construction, are easy to secure between exposed ceiling members. Cut-in or remodeling models are also available—they slip into, then clip onto, a hole cut in an existing ceiling.

Surface-mounted fixtures include mirror-side wall sconces, makeup lights, ceiling globes and pendants, undercabinet task lights, and decorative flourishes like neon or rope lights.

Lighting controls make life more flexible. Dimmers allow you to dial in any light level from full throttle to a near fireside glow. Timer switches police children's bath lights and fans, or turn on a heater so the room's toasty for that 5 A.M. wake-up call. Motion sensors switch lights on when you enter the room.

SURFACE-MOUNTED BAR

WALL SCONCES

Storage *Solutions*

IN THE OLD DAYS, "bathroom storage" meant a clunky medicine cabinet mounted above a pedestal or wall-hung lavatory sink. Then along came boxy vanities, and the bathroom acquired a bank of drawers alongside the plumbing. As bathrooms morph into grooming centers, exercise gyms, and spas, their storage needs and configurations are also changing.

One or more base cabinets may still form the backbone of the modern storage scheme, but many bath storage areas now resemble kitchen plans, their design integrated with that of mirrors, sink, lighting, and backsplash. Perhaps you'll want to curve a custom unit around a corner, add an island, or plan a floor-to-ceiling storage "pantry."

Or you may choose to head in the opposite direction, following the trend toward free-standing or unfitted vanities that look like traditional furniture. Such pieces, either custom or recycled, can be tailored to fit nearly any style, and they work especially well with today's above-counter sinks.

The good old medicine cabinet comes in stylish new versions, many with mirrors and built-in light fixtures. Or you might consider a recessed built-in with a seamless, touch-

Left: Here's a fun twist on the unfitted look. A central storage tower rises between matching open sink separates, each with a shelf below.

latch mirror or two above. It needn't be sinkside: recessed cabinets and niches can add storage and display space elsewhere without intruding on limited floor space.

Custom storage towers and shallow cabinets take up the slack, especially if a pedestal or wall sink has replaced a standard deck-mounted sink—and the vanity space below. Built-in room dividers add storage while defining compartmentalized layouts. Open shelves complement both casual and country designs and add display space, too. Other options include freestanding armoires and flea-market finds such as chests, bureaus, and baskets. There's also a growing list of modular wall-system components that adapt well to bathrooms.

Help your storage units work harder with the new generation of add-ons and accessories, from door racks and drawer organizers to pullout shelves, lazy Susans and turntables, and even TV lifts. And don't overlook hooks, towel bars, and other such practical finishing touches.

Top right: Don't forget display space. These narrow shelf ledges wrap the tub walls and form a happy, humid home for seaside creatures—though they'd probably prefer salt water.

Bottom right: Think furniture, not cabinets—like this chest of drawers with a sleek vessel sink on top. The plumbing runs right through the base of the chest.

Right: A converted cedar potting bench makes a clever alternative to the standard closed vanity. The owner cut a hole for a self-rimmed sink, added the towel bar and paper holder, and finished up with marine varnish.

Left: These clean white built-ins look like traditional pieces of furniture. They provide plenty of drawer space and such decorative touches as glass display shelves, arched soffit trim, fluted vertical pilasters, and a beadboard back.

Above: A tile-topped bureau with scroll-cut legs warms this bathroom space, echoing the style of the bedroom beyond.

Left: A steel U-beam takes on an unexpected new life as a sturdy wall-hung vanity, with room for both sink and towels.

Facing page: A built-in wall tower does the lion's share of storage work in this bathroom. Closed cubbies join with open-fronted compartments and "drawer-front" double pullouts to provide huge amounts of storage space—and great looks.

Left: Divide and conquer. This toilet partition doubles as towel rack and display space.

Above: A classic white wall unit turns a triple play as glass-front medicine cabinet, towel rack, and display shelf.

Left: How do you get back storage lost to the vanity? This console sink is flanked by some seriously hard-working company, including twin base drawer units and enclosed, stepped-back upper towers.

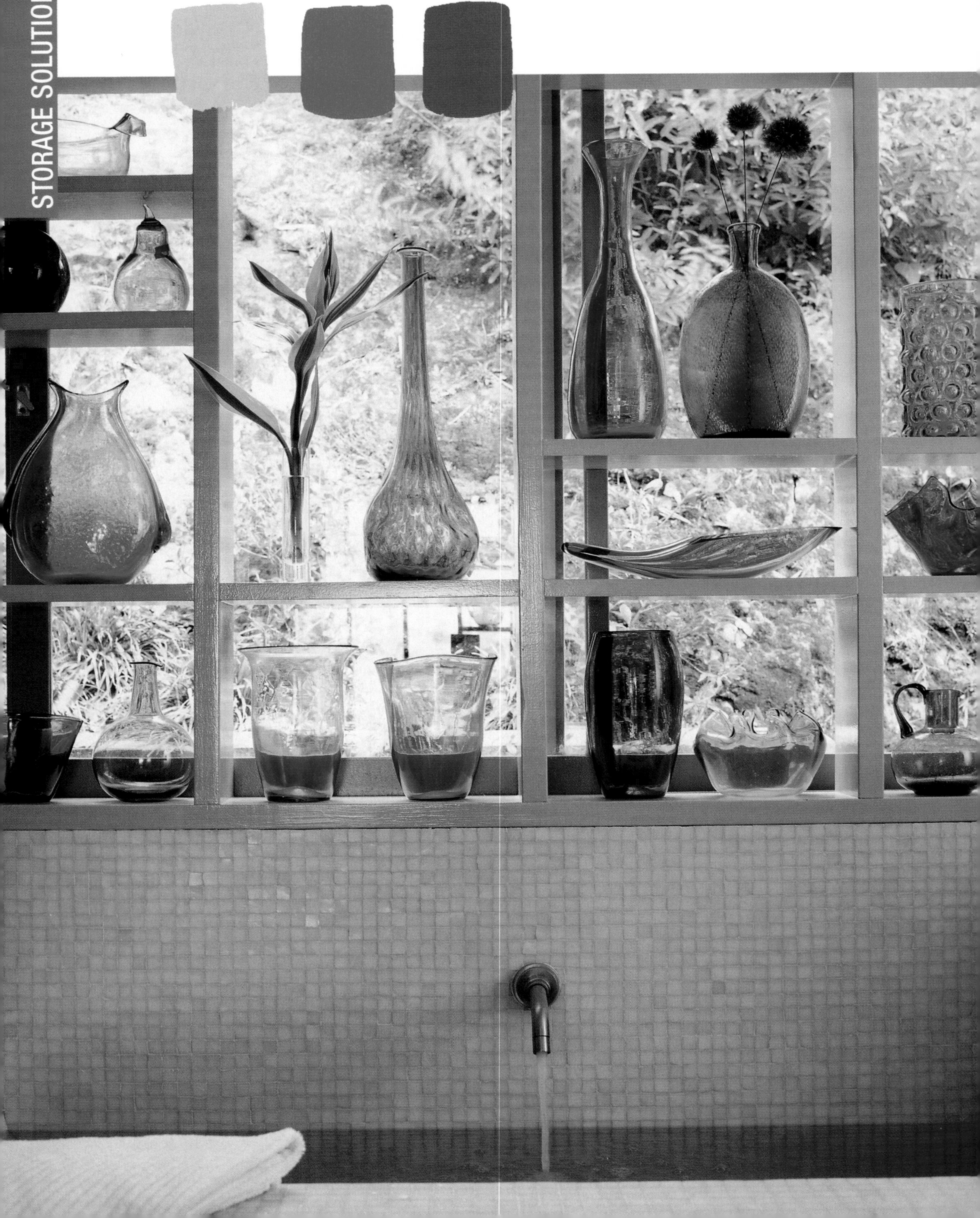

Left: A bright red storage unit defines this room while providing door-fronted compartments below and wicker baskets on open shelves above.

Facing page: A scattering of shelf alcoves passes light through a collection of colored glass vases and vessels—and provides a touch of tubside privacy as well.

Above: Uncluttered "floating" shelves seemingly hover in front of decoratively combed walls; they're anchored by invisible cantilevered brackets.

Left: A tub alcove makes room for a bank of built-ins, including open shelves, cubbies, closed lower cabinets, and glass-fronted upper shelves.

Below: Looking for a twist on the traditional medicine cabinet? This one is hidden behind a thin, wood-framed mirror that slides sideways on wall-mounted drawer guides.

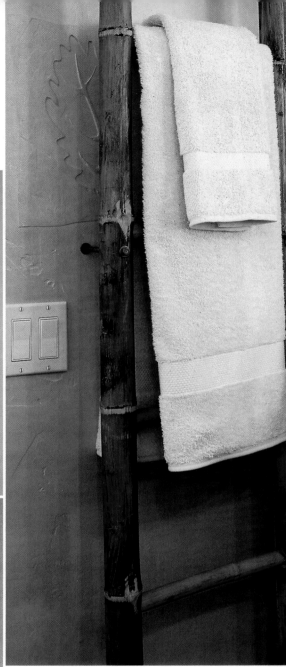

Above: All sorts of found objects can hold towels and add interest. Bolts driven through the upright pieces into wall studs turned this bamboo ladder into a first-rate towel bar.

Left: Kitchens often include appliance garages for keeping frequently needed odds and ends out of sight; why not baths? This tambour-doored alcove is mounted sideways to save space. Note the built-in power outlet inside the garage.

Above: Here's another take on the appliance garage. This one, in a backsplash recess, features hinged bifold doors. The hideaway divides the floating limestone counter into two stations.

Far left: Starfish hooks swim in a row across the wainscoting in a playful bathroom layout.

Near left: Iron wine-bottle holders are another "found" idea for towel storage.

SHOPPER'S GUIDE

All about *Cabinets*

Though the trend is toward bath storage that's more free-form, your storage scheme will probably still be anchored by one or more base or wall cabinets. Here's what to look for.

Traditional or Euro-style?

The first decision you'll need to make is whether you want framed or frameless cabinetry in your bathroom.

Traditional cabinets mask the raw front edges of each box with a 1-by-2 "faceframe." Doors and drawers then fit in one of three ways: flush (inset); partially offset, with a lip; or overlaying the frame. In all three versions, the frame is visible, giving you the nice look of real wood. But the frame takes up space and reduces the opening size, so drawers or slide-out accessories must be significantly smaller than the full width of the cabinet.

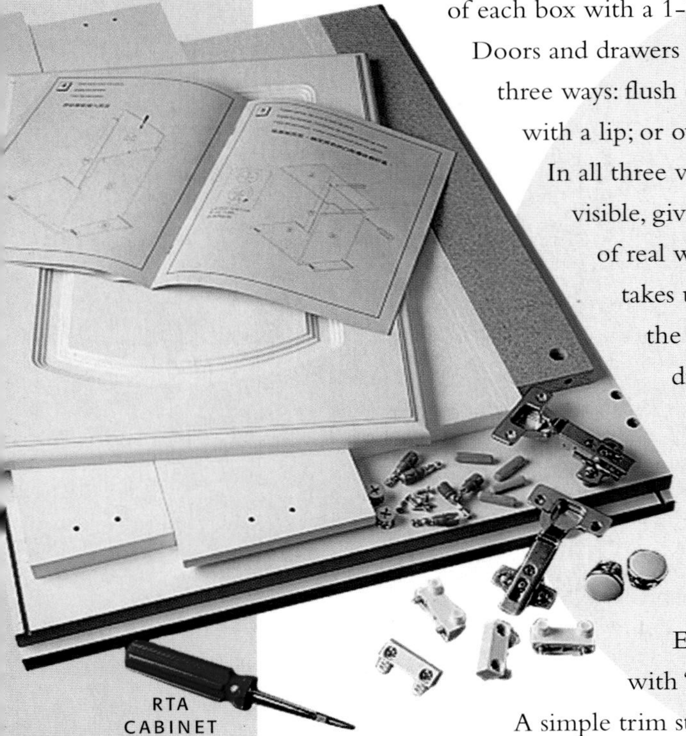

Europeans came up with "frameless" cabinets. A simple trim strip covers raw edges, which butt directly against one another.

Doors and drawers, usually overlay style, often fit to within ⅛ inch of each other, revealing just a thin sliver of the trim. Drawers and other interior components can be sized practically to the full dimensions of the box. Another big difference: frameless cabinets often rest on a separate toespace pedestal, or plinth. This allows you to set counter heights specifically to your liking, stack base units, or make use of space at floor level.

Basic options

Standard bathroom base cabinets, or vanities, are sold in 3-inch increments from 9 to 48 inches wide. They're typically sized smaller than kitchen cabinets—about 32 inches tall by 21 inches deep. Want something bigger? Look to kitchen lines, which normally are 34½ inches tall by 24 inches deep.

A recent development, the RTA (ready-to-assemble) cabinet, costs even less than other stock units, but it requires some basic tools and elbow grease to put together. An RTA stock cabinet is shown at left.

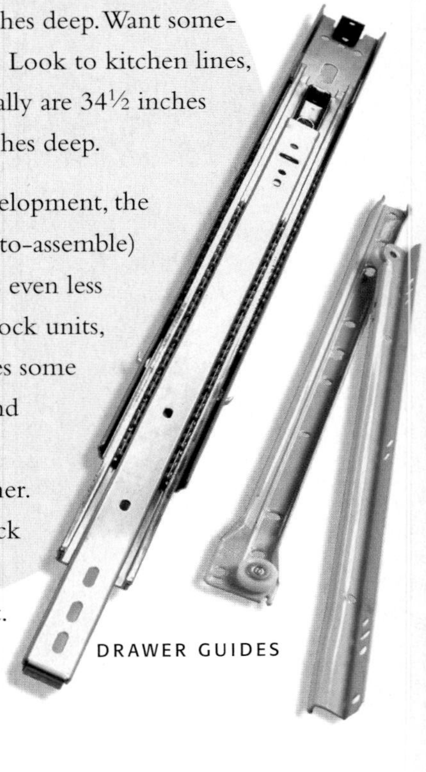

RTA CABINET

DRAWER GUIDES

Judging quality

To spot-check the quality of a cabinet, first examine the drawers—they'll take more of a beating than any other part of your cabinets. Several drawer designs are shown at right. You'll pay a premium for features such as solid-wood drawer boxes, sturdy dovetail joints, and full-extension, ball-bearing guides.

The simplest, least expensive door option is often a flat or "slab" design, popular for seamless European cabinets. Frame-and-panel doors are more traditional and come in many versions, including raised-panel (both real and simulated), arched panel, beaded panel, and recessed or flat panel.

Door hinges are critical hardware elements. European or "invisible" cup hinges are the most trouble-free; consider these unless you need the period look of surface hardware. Check for adjustability; you should be able to reset hinges with the cabinets in place.

Most cabinet boxes are made from sheet products like plywood, particleboard (plain or laminated), or medium-density fiberboard. (Though solid lumber is sometimes used, it is more often saved for the doors and drawers.)

Hardwood plywood is surfaced with attractive wood veneers on both face and back; the higher the face grade, the more you'll pay. Particleboard costs less, weighs more, and is both weaker and more prone to warping and moisture damage than plywood. Particleboard vanities generally are faced with high-pressure laminate or with a softer material called melamine. Medium-density fiberboard (MDF) is a denser, furniture-grade particleboard that is available with high-quality hardwood veneers.

DRAWER DETAILS

FACEFRAME CABINET

FRAMELESS CABINET

Elegant *Extras*

AS LIFE SPEEDS UP, many of us treasure quiet time. So for some people the bathroom is becoming a down-time retreat, complete with such extras as a soaking tub and comfortable sitting space. Standard living-room features—fireplaces, media centers, and wet bars—are moving in. Even a small space has room for a few amenities—a heated towel bar, a toespace heater, a flat-screen TV.

Master suites blur the distinction between bed and bath, blending separate zones for bathing, grooming, dressing, working, and relaxing in a private part of the house. The desire for repose may tempt you to add a comfortable couch or chair, built-in bookcases, a reading lamp, and perhaps a corner wet bar or breakfast counter. Bring in art and collectibles, and maybe built-in speakers connected to a central home audio system (it's a good idea to have at least a separate volume control within reach). Or indulge in a large-screen TV or full-blown home theater serving both bed and bath areas.

If you'd like a traditional makeup table, you will need to find a spot for it out of the main flow. Plan a lowered counter, about desk height, so that it's comfortable to use when you are seated. Where will you store cosmetics, jewelry, and accessories? What mirrors and lighting will you need? Do you want an auxiliary sink?

Left: It's a garden, it's a pocket deck, and it's a shower, all opening up right off the bedroom.

A walk-in closet can neatly combine clothes storage with a dressing area. Or opt for modular drawers and pullouts, or a freestanding closet or armoire, and add a built-in or free-standing bench. If space permits, this area can serve as a bridge between bedroom and bath. Good ventilation, especially for areas adjacent to a shower or tub, is crucial.

Workday add-on possibilities abound. What about a compact desk, a re-cessed bookcase, and a high-speed computer connection? Or how about some space for those pre-computer tasks that remain with us—a stacked washer-dryer combo and a fold-down ironing board, or a sewing center that stows away behind sliding or bifold doors? Manufacturers of modular wall-systems offer many options.

Blur the boundaries between indoors and out with sliding or French doors, an outdoor shower, a greenhouse, or a small courtyard garden—most plants love the heat and humidity your nearby bath can offer. Besides bringing the outdoors in, these extras help stretch space in otherwise cramped quarters.

Top right: Formally dressed cabinets house some extra goodies, including an in-drawer breakfast bar and a pullout TV.

Bottom right: A spacious dressing area, in a transition zone right off the bath proper, sports generous closet space, stylish drawer banks, a built-in bench, and a beautiful decorative-glass window.

How about a really cozy fireside soak? A see-through gas fireplace links the bathroom space with this master suite's bedroom.

Top: A formal makeup area houses mirrors, windows, and traditional wall sconces, plus its own sink and toespace heater.

Above: This built-in makeup center wraps around the corner to join a cushioned daybed bench to the left.

Right: White laminate built-ins present a seamless Euro-style face of flush-front doors and drawers. Mirrors add space-stretching flash to an otherwise blank wall.

Below: Modular units like this beautifully made closet system offer lots of opportunities to customize space. Drawers, pullouts, rods, and even a swing-down rack let you mix and match the dressing-area components of your dreams.

Above: A cedar-and-granite grooming area, complete with twin sinks and expansive mirrors, occupies one wall of a comfortable master suite. A striking cedar storage wall divides bed from bath and also works, on the bedroom side, as a headboard.

Left: Beyond this spacious bath and dressing area lies a no-holds-barred workout room, complete with its own auxiliary air-conditioning system.

Facing page: Want a sauna? You just need cedar paneling and benches, a sauna heater, and a close-fitting door—and, most important, the space in which to put it. From here, it's a short stroll to the tile-lined shower.

Below: A children's bath shares space with the laundry, consolidating dirt in one location. Stacking washer-dryer units allow you to shoehorn a laundry into some pretty tight spaces—even behind a bank of cabinet fronts.

Finishing *Touches*

SOAP DISPENSER

OPTICAL
MAKEUP
MIRROR

In bath design, as in life, it's often the little things that count. Don't forget to include in your plan those subtle amenities that can furnish the delightful finishing touches to your bathroom.

Commercial accessory lines are more complete than ever; some towel bars, hooks, and tissue holders even correspond with faucet handles. Additional matchables may include soap dishes, toothbrush holders, cup holders, cabinet pulls, switch plates, mirrors, light fixtures, and decorative wall tiles. And how about a pedestal sink or bathtub that's part of the same collection?

Other popular amenities include adjustable makeup mirrors (typically in 3× or 5× power), with or without optical glass and internal illumination; shaving mirrors for the shower; heated towel bars; and home-entertainment components (TVs, built-in speakers, remote control panels).

Want to stretch your storage space? Add-on cabinet inserts are available for just about any use imaginable in the bathroom. Some of them simply slip inside doors or drawers; others are screwed or bolted to cabinet interiors. If you're outfitting a pre-existing cabinet, be sure to check the sizes and clearances required for add-ons.

CABINET PULLS

COORDINATED
ACCESSORY
LINE

HAND-PAINTED SWITCH PLATE

TOWEL RING

FABRIC SHOWER CURTAIN

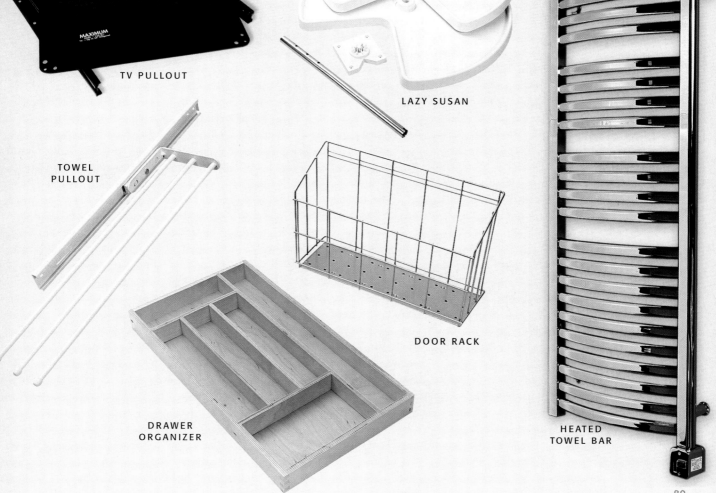

TV PULLOUT

LAZY SUSAN

TOWEL
PULLOUT

DOOR RACK

DRAWER
ORGANIZER

HEATED
TOWEL BAR

MAXIMUM

89

How to DO IT

READY TO MAKE YOUR NEW BATH a reality? Behind those shiny fixtures and gleaming tiles are codes and clearances, critical dimensions, and effective design principles. Use this chapter as a planning workbook. First we help you evaluate your existing bathroom. Then we guide you through layout and design basics, and we finish by taking a look at the remodeling process and the professionals who can help you. Before you know it, you'll be building the bath of your dreams.

Taking *Stock*

BEFORE YOU START SHOPPING, take time to assess what you already have. A clear, accurate base map—like the one shown on page 94—will be your best planning tool. Your base map will also help you communicate with both design professionals and showroom personnel. In addition, the questionnaire on page 95 can help you analyze your options.

Measuring the space

To make your bathroom survey, you'll need either a folding wooden rule or a steel measuring tape. The folding rule (shown above right) is the pro's choice: it stays rigid when extended and is good for "inside" measurements.

Start by sketching out your present layout (don't worry about scale), doodling in windows, doors, fixtures, and other features. Then measure each wall at counter height. Here's an example, using a hypothetical bathroom with bathtub and door along one wall: beginning at one corner, measure the distance to the outer edge of the door, from there to the opposite door edge, from this edge to the bathtub, and finally across the bathtub to the corner. After you finish measuring the wall, total the incremental figures; then check the result by taking a single overall measurement from corner

Left: Unfitted bath layouts are flexible and help stretch space. Pedestal sinks and freestanding storage pieces are both traditional choices.

FOLDING WOODEN RULE

to corner. The two figures should match exactly.

Continue measuring around the room, and then measure the floor-to-ceiling height of each wall in the same manner. Do the facing walls agree? If not, something's out of level or out of plumb; find out what it is. To check the corners, use a carpenter's square directly or employ the 3-4-5 method: measure along the wall 3 feet from a corner in one direction, and 4 feet in the other direction, and connect these two points with a straightedge. If the connecting distance measures 5 feet, the corner is square.

Top right: This evolving children's bath makes room for collectibles from its earlier years.

Bottom right: No room for another full-size bath? In temperate climes, consider an outdoor shower, saving indoor space for other fixtures and amenities.

ARCHITECTURAL SYMBOLS

WALL

WINDOW

POCKET DOOR

DOOR SWING

DUPLEX WALL OUTLET

WALL SWITCH/ CEILING FIXTURE

WALL FIXTURE

CENTERLINE, PLUMBING

A SAMPLE BASE MAP

Making a base map

Now draw your bathroom to scale. All you really need is a straight-edge—ruler, T-square, or triangle—and some standard drafting paper with ¼-inch squares. An architect's ruler is helpful but not really necessary. Most bathroom designers use a ½-inch scale (1/24 actual size); that's two drafting-paper squares per foot.

Tape the corners of the paper to a smooth work surface, and then use the straightedge to plot all horizontal and vertical lines; make right angles exact. If you have a compass, use it to indicate door swings.

If you prefer, you can make your map with one of the newer computer software programs—you won't need anything complicated. (You can, of course, use the same program to draw your new bathroom, too.)

The sample base map shown above includes centerlines to sink plumbing and electrical symbols for outlets, switches, and fixtures. It's also helpful to note the direction of joists and to identify any bearing walls (see pages 116–117). Sketch in other features that might affect your plans.

Left: A complete kit of mapping tools includes a pencil, a T-square, a triangle, and an architect's ruler.

TWENTY
Questions

1. What's your main reason for changing your bathroom?

2. How many people will be using the room? How tall is each one? Is the bath to be used by an elderly or disabled person?

3. Do you like compartmentalized layouts or a more open look? Will more than one person be using the room at the same time?

4. How's the traffic flow? Is there adequate clearance between fixtures? Can existing doors and windows be relocated to improve traffic patterns, if necessary?

5. What secondary activity areas would you like to include—dressing area, makeup table, entertainment center, exercise facilities, laundry?

6. What new fixtures, if any, are you planning? Is the toilet where you want it? Is the shower head at a convenient height? Are fixtures and fittings easy to clean? Do they waste water or energy?

7. What style would you like for your new bathroom—high-tech, country, or Arts and Crafts, for example? How does that style relate to nearby rooms and to your home's exterior?

8. What color combinations do you prefer? And what fixture finish do you like: white, pastel, stronger color?

9. Evaluate your bathroom's surfaces. Are they damaged or dated?

10. Is your present bathroom safe? Are surfaces slippery? Is the tub easy to get into and out of? Are electrical circuits protected by ground fault circuit interrupters (GFCIs)?

11. What kinds of light fixtures do you like? What natural light sources are possible?

12. What type of heating system do you have? Is it adequate?

13. How's the climate in your bathroom after a steamy shower? Would you prefer natural or mechanical ventilation, or both?

14. What are your bathroom storage requirements? Do you like the idea of open storage and display?

15. Are you planning any structural changes, such as a greenhouse window or an addition to the room? Is there a full basement, crawl space, or concrete slab beneath the bathroom?

16. What's the amp rating of your electrical service?

17. What kind of water-supply pipes do you have? How's your water pressure? Do any pipes leak?

18. Are you willing and able to do any or all of the demolition or building yourself?

19. How long do you have to complete the project?

20. What budget figure do you have in mind?

You'll want to take an inventory of your present bathroom in order to judge how you want to change it. Used with your base map, your responses to the questions at left will also provide a good starting point for a discussion with architects, designers, or showroom personnel. Write your answers on a separate sheet of paper, adding any other preferences or dislikes that come to mind. Then gather your notes, any clippings you've collected, and a copy of your base map, and you're ready to begin planning your new bathroom.

Layout
Basics

NOW COMES THE FUN PART—actually planning your new bathroom. While brainstorming, it helps to have some basic layout schemes in mind. The floor plans shown here are both practical and efficient. Keep in mind that these layouts can be combined, adapted, or expanded to meet your needs. For many more examples, see "Great Spaces," beginning on page 8.

Powder room

This two-fixture room, also known as a guest bath or half-bath, contains a toilet and a sink and perhaps limited storage space. Fixtures can be side by side or on opposite walls, depending on the shape of the room. Very small sinks are available for extra-tight spaces. The door should swing open against a wall, clear of fixtures. A pocket door may be the ideal solution where space is at a premium.

Because the powder room has high visibility but sees only sporadic use, it's a good place to enjoy more decorative but perhaps less practical finishes, such as copper, glass, or upholstery. Light fixtures can be jazzier here, too.

Consideration should be given to privacy. Preferably, a powder room will open off a hallway—not a living, family, or dining space. Aim for even, flattering mirror-side lighting. Check that there's adequate ventilation.

Left: Powder rooms present a canvas for some modern art—in this case, a stainless-steel vessel sink, a wall-mounted faucet, wood and concrete walls, and a seamless built-in mirror.

Family bath

The family bath usually contains three fixtures—a toilet, a sink, and a shower or combination tub/shower. The arrangement of these fixtures varies, depending on the size and shape of the room. Family baths often are configured with fixtures clustered on one or both sides of a center "corridor." Such a layout should be at least 5 by 7 feet.

"Compartmentalizing" or separating fixture areas enables more than one family member to use the bathroom at once. A common arrangement is to isolate the toilet and shower (and perhaps a small secondary sink) from the basin and grooming area.

Children's bath

Ideally, the children's bathroom is next to their bedrooms so that each user has easy access. When several children are involved, consider doors directly into the bathroom from two bedrooms, or shared bathing and toilet facilities with an individual sink and dressing area for each child. Color-coding of drawers, towel hooks, and other storage areas can minimize territorial battles. A pullout step below the vanity helps a growing user reach the sink.

Children's baths require special attention to safety (see page 111). Timers on the light switch and the fan will keep your electrical bill down. Plastic-laminate counters and cabinets are durable and easy to clean.

SAMPLE BATHROOM LAYOUTS

POWDER ROOM
5' BY 5'

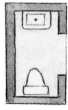

POWDER ROOM
3' BY 6'

POWDER ROOM
4' BY 4'6"

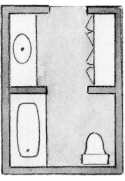

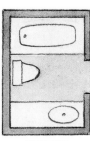

FAMILY BATH
5' BY 7'

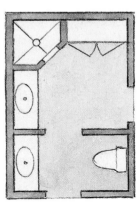

FAMILY BATH
7' BY 11'

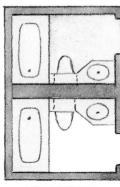

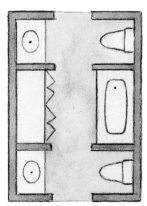

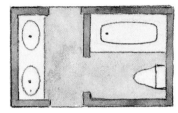

FAMILY BATH
8' BY 12'

BACK-TO-BACK BATHS
5' BY 7' EACH

CHILDREN'S BATH
8' BY 12'

CHILDREN'S BATH
6' BY 10'

Master bath/suite

The master bath has become much more than just a place to take a quick shower and run a comb through your hair. Today's multiroom master suite can also be a personal oasis reflecting the personalities and interests of its owners. Besides sink, toilet, and bathing facilities, it may include an oversize whirlpool tub, a walk-in shower, and a bidet. The outdoor area just beyond such a bath is a natural place for a spa, sunbathing deck, or private garden.

Here are some "extras" to consider as you plan your new space. Be sure that you provide adequate ventilation to prevent water damage (from both splashes and condensation) to delicate objects and equipment.

- Grooming center
- Dressing area, walk-in closet
- Exercise room
- Entertainment center
- Art gallery
- Reading nook
- Breakfast bar
- Laundry area
- Greenhouse
- Outdoor shower and deck
- Home office or computer niche
- Steam shower and/or sauna
- Master control panel for home lighting/intercom/security system

MASTER BATH LAYOUTS

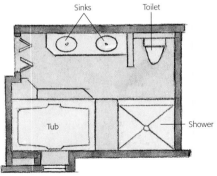

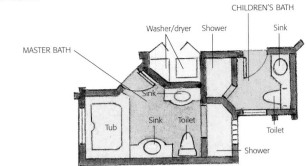

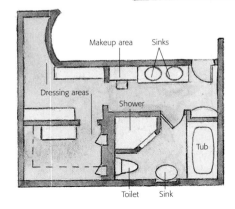

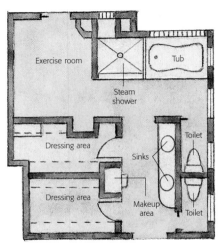

Above: Master suites roll bed and bath areas into one private retreat. This suite features a spa alcove, makeup and dressing areas, and a spacious exercise room beyond.

Arranging *Fixtures*

THE MORE FACTS YOU HAVE, the easier it will be to plan your layout. You'll keep costs down if you select a layout that uses the existing plumbing (see page 118). In general, you can move a sink a few inches or add a second sink with only minor plumbing changes. You can also extend existing drain lines if the distance from the vent is within the maximum distance allowed by your local code.

If you're adding on to your house, try to locate the new bathroom near an existing bathroom or the kitchen. It's also most economical to arrange fixtures against one or two walls, eliminating the need for additional plumbing lines.

Begin by positioning the largest unit—the bathtub or shower—within your floor plan, allowing space for convenient access, cleaning, and (if needed) bathing a child. Next place the sink (or sinks). The most frequently used fixture in the bathroom, the sink ideally will be out of the traffic pattern. Allow ample room in front for reaching below the sink, and give plenty of elbow room at the sides.

Locate the toilet (and bidet, if you are installing one) away from the door. Often the toilet is placed beside the tub or shower. A toilet and bidet should be next to each other.

Don't forget to take into consideration the swing radius for windows and doors.

Left: Think corners! For example, a corner shower like this one can help solve layout puzzles.

Standard clearances

Building codes and industry guide-lines specify certain clearances between, beside, and in front of bathroom fixtures to allow enough room for use, cleaning, and repair. To help in your initial planning, check the minimum clearances shown on this page. If an elderly or disabled person will use the space, increase these clearances as much as possible (see "Universal Design," page 103).

You can generally locate side-by-side fixtures closer together than fixtures positioned opposite each other. If a sink is opposite a bathtub or toilet, keep a minimum of 30 inches between them, preferably more.

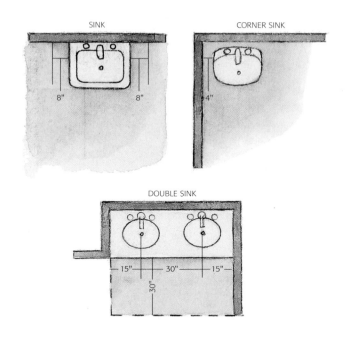

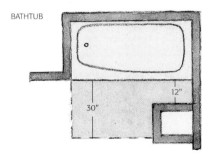

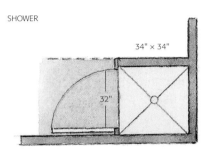

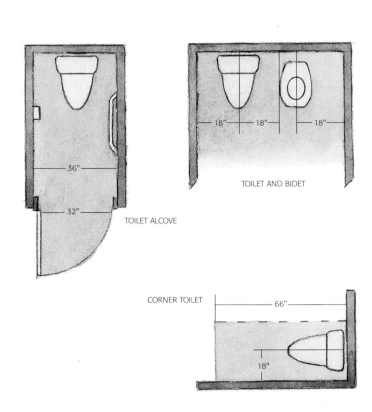

STANDARD HEIGHTS

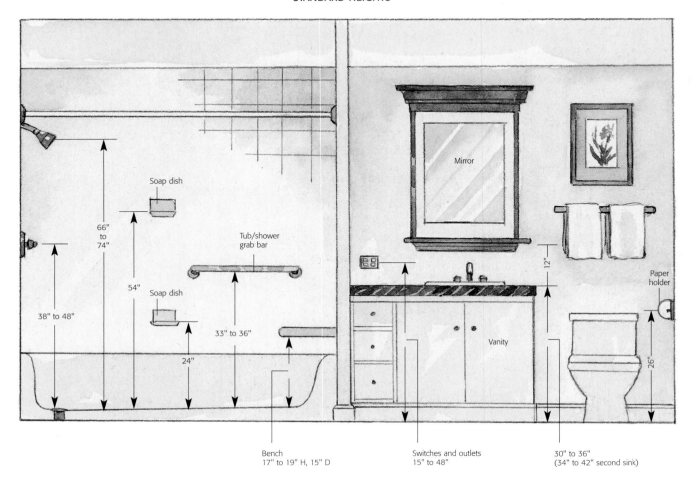

66" to 74"

54"

38" to 48"

Soap dish

Soap dish

Tub/shower grab bar

33" to 36"

24"

Mirror

Vanity

12"

Paper holder

26"

Bench
17" to 19" H, 15" D

Switches and outlets
15" to 48"

30" to 36"
(34" to 42" second sink)

Going vertical

Shown above are standard heights for cabinets and countertops, shower heads and valves, grab bars and other accessories. If you and others using the bathroom are especially tall or short, you may wish to customize the room to your own requirements. When planning such a change, keep one eye on your home's resale value: will potential buyers find these alterations as convenient as you do?

If you're planning multiple sinks, the first should be no higher than 36 inches off the floor. If desired, the second may be between 34 and 42 inches above the floor, depending on the height of the user.

Experimenting with your ideas

To visualize possible layouts, draw scale outlines of fixtures and cabinets you're considering and cut them out. (Photocopy your outlines to give yourself multiple copies to play around with.) Move the cutouts around on copies of your base map to find the best arrangement. Then draw the shapes onto the plan.

You can also make layouts using a design kit that includes graph paper and ready-made scale cutouts. Another possibility is a computer software program specifically designed for creating floor plans. The computer makes it easy to try and compare many different layouts.

UNIVERSAL *Design*

Most bathrooms are set up with healthy adults in mind. But according to the National Kitchen & Bath Association, or NKBA, fewer than 15 percent of bathroom users fit that description. If you're remodeling a bath for an elderly or disabled person—or if you're simply looking down the road for yourself—you'll want to be aware of the growing trend toward "universal" or barrier-free design.

Special heights, clearances, and room dimensions may be required. To accommodate a wheelchair, for instance, the room's openings—from door to shower to toilet enclosure—should be at least 34 inches wide. You'll also need to plan turn-around areas near fixtures; a 5-foot diameter is ideal. The bathroom door should swing outward to allow easy movement in and out of the room. The

shower should be curbless so that a wheelchair can roll in unobstructed.

User-friendly heights are critical. A sink must be no more than 34 inches from the floor, and significant storage areas should be between 15 and 48 inches high. It's important to leave an open space below the sink to allow knee room for a seated user; plan to cover under-sink plumbing. Handles, switches, and other controls should be no more than 48 inches off the floor.

Exchange standard doorknobs, faucet handles, and cabinet hardware for levers and pulls that can be operated with one closed hand or a wrist. Grab bars are a must in shower, tub, and toilet areas. Plan a seat inside the shower or tub. Extra lighting may also be needed.

Below: Universal bath accessories include a tub seat and grab bar (top photo) and a fold-down shower seat (bottom).

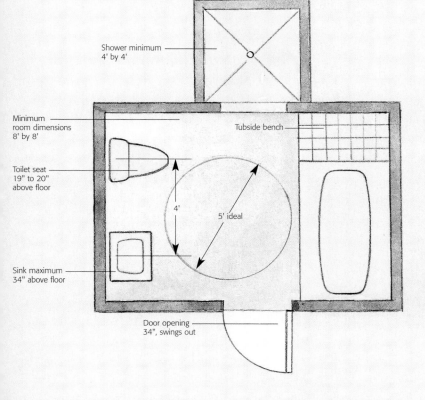

Shower minimum 4' by 4'

Minimum room dimensions 8' by 8'

Tubside bench

Toilet seat 19" to 20" above floor

4'

5' ideal

Sink maximum 34" above floor

Door opening 34", swings out

Setting *a Style*

WITH YOUR BASIC FLOOR PLAN IN MIND, start to fine-tune your decorating scheme. Wall and ceiling coverings, flooring, and even fixtures and fittings are powerful tools for evoking style and mood. Your choices in color, pattern, texture, scale, and shape will all help you achieve a particular style effect. Here we introduce some reliable design concepts—use them as starting points, not strict rules.

What's your style?

A decorating style has physical characteristics that identify it with a particular region, era, or artistic movement—Victorian, Southwestern, Arts and Crafts, Art Deco, and so on. Because certain colors, materials, and decorative motifs are linked to historic decorating styles, they can be used to evoke a period feeling—or simply to personalize and add dignity to a bland modern room.

Here are some examples of styles:

- Period (such as Georgian, French, early American)

- Regional (Southwestern, Spanish, New England)

- Country (rustic, English, French)

- Romantic

- Contemporary (also high-tech, minimalist)

Left: This powder room is electric with eclectic color, texture, and mixed materials.

- Retro (Mission, Art Deco, fifties)

- Global

- Eclectic

You'll find examples of these various influences throughout this book. That said, rarely are styles slavish replicas of historic designs. More typically, designers select elements that echo the mood of a particular period or look. What matters is that you choose a mood you find sympathetic and comfortable. And if the bathroom is linked to adjoining spaces, its look should match or at least complement the style of those spaces.

If you're stuck, think opposites. For example, do you like modern or classic lines; a formal or homey feel; coordinated pieces or one-of-a-kind collectibles? Should comfort or efficiency get the nod?

Style often starts with one element you've fallen in love with—then other choices are a matter of how they match up. That starting point could be an antique pedestal sink, a Japanese soaking tub, a freestanding pine chest, some Art Deco tiles, or a pair of hand-blown Italian-glass sconces. When in doubt, go shopping!

Top right: Stone, a soaking tub, and a tranquil view are hallmarks of a naturalistic, Asian-influenced bath.

Bottom right: Formal as can be, this master suite combines classic touches with a fully modern cast of components.

Line, shape, and scale

Three visual keys to planning a balanced, pleasing bathroom design are line, shape, and scale. You'll need to think about each of these elements—along with texture and pattern—to achieve the look you want. Color is crucial, too; for guidelines, see page 109.

Most bathrooms incorporate many different types of lines—vertical, horizontal, diagonal, curved, and angular—but usually one predominates. Vertical lines give a sense of height, horizontals impart width, diagonals suggest movement, and curved and angular lines contribute a feeling of grace and dynamism.

Try an elevation (head-on) sketch of your proposed bathroom. How do the vertical lines created by the shower or tub unit, cabinets, vanity, windows, doors, and mirrors fit together? Do the tops of windows, shower surround, door, and mirror align horizontally?

Continuity and compatibility in shape also contribute to a unified design. Study the shapes created by doorways, windows, countertops, fixtures, and other elements. Look at patterns in your flooring, wall coverings, shower curtain, and towels. Are they different or similar? If similar, are they boringly repetitive? Think of ways to complement existing shapes or add compatible new ones. For example, you might echo an arch over a recessed bathtub in the shape of a doorway, or perhaps in shelf trim.

When the scale of bathroom elements is proportionate to the overall size of the room, the design feels harmonious. A small bath seems even smaller if equipped with large fixtures and a large vanity. But the same bath can look larger, or at least in scale, if fitted with space-saving fixtures, a petite vanity, tiny mosaic tiles, and open shelves.

Left: Rectangles are at work here, including the carefully placed wall sink, storage cabinets, the mirror, and even a rectangular wall toilet and overhead light fixture.

Texture and pattern

A bathroom's surface materials may include many different textures—from glossy countertops to sturdy but soft-looking wood cabinets and rustically irregular terra-cotta tile flooring.

Rough textures absorb light, make colors look duller, and lend a feeling of informality. Smooth textures, on the other hand, reflect light and tend to suggest elegance or modernity. Using similar textures helps unify a design and create a mood.

Pattern choices should harmonize with the predominant style of the room. Although we usually associate patterns with wall coverings or tile, even natural substances such as wood and stone create patterns.

While variety in texture and pattern adds interest, too much variety can be overstimulating. It's usually best to let a strong feature or a dominating pattern be the focus of your design and to choose other surfaces to complement rather than compete with it. In general, the smaller the bathroom, the subtler you should be.

Top right: Even understated materials can add pattern and texture. Tiny mosaic tiles line this shower and spa; they're echoed in terrazzo on both the floor and the countertop.

Bottom right: Texture, pattern, and color combine in a vivid art mosaic. For full effect, contrast bold strokes against a more neutral backdrop.

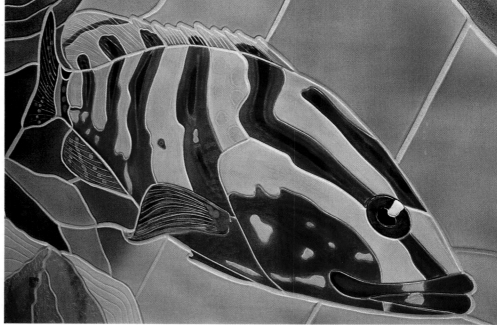

A monochromatic color scheme wraps this stylish powder room in warm gold tones. Texture provides the contrast, as seen in the tissue-papered walls and gilded mirror frame.

All about color

The size and orientation of your bathroom, your personal preferences, and the mood you want to create all affect color selection. Light colors reflect light, making walls appear to recede; thus a small bath decorated in light colors feels more spacious. Dark colors absorb light and seem to lower a ceiling or shorten a narrow room.

Depending on the orientation of your bathroom, you may want to use warm or cool colors to balance the quality of the light. While oranges, yellows, and colors with a red tone impart a feeling of warmth, they also contract space. Blues, greens, and colors with a blue tone make an area seem cooler—and larger.

When considering colors for a small bathroom, remember that too much contrast has the same effect as dark color: it reduces the sense of expansiveness. Contrasting colors work well for adding accents or drawing attention to interesting structural elements. But to conceal a problem feature, it's best to use a single color throughout the area.

The key to understanding color combinations is the color wheel. But today's palettes rarely use the pure colors on the wheel; instead, they feature low-intensity versions of these hues, as shown at right.

A light, *monochromatic* color scheme (using different shades of a single color) tends to feel restful and serene. So do neutrals, which rely primarily on whites, grays, and blacks. A favorite color trick for small bathrooms is to combine one low-intensity color or neutral with white.

FULL-INTENSITY COLORS

LOW-INTENSITY COLORS

Analogous schemes consist of colors that are side by side on the color wheel. Red, red-orange, and orange are analogous, and so are blue, blue-violet, and violet. An analogous scheme gains punch from a mix of patterns and textures.

Complementary combinations are made up of colors that lie directly opposite each other on the color wheel. Red and green are complements, as are yellow-orange and blue-violet. Remember that a color scheme with contrasting colors can be overpowering unless you choose laid-back versions of those colors.

For a look at some effective color palettes, see pages 124–125.

Making a design board

Before you commit to any design decisions, you will want to live with them for a while. As you narrow your style selections, create a design board to see how your choices work together. Color charts for various fixtures are readily available, as are paint chips, tiles, fabric swatches, and wallpaper and flooring samples.

Natural light from windows and skylights will influence your color palette. Remember, too, that the placement of light fixtures, and the kinds of bulbs used in them, will have an effect on color. For details on lighting, see pages 112–113.

What about *Storage?*

AFTER PLOTTING THE PLACEMENT OF FIXTURES, plan your storage spaces. While a powder room has few requirements, a family bath should include storage space for each family member, as well as places to keep cleaning supplies, paper products, soap, and incidentals. Today's master suite may double as a dressing room or a nighttime retreat, so take time to consider these needs.

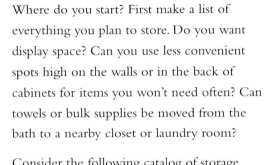

Where do you start? First make a list of everything you plan to store. Do you want display space? Can you use less convenient spots high on the walls or in the back of cabinets for items you won't need often? Can towels or bulk supplies be moved from the bath to a nearby closet or laundry room?

Consider the following catalog of storage weapons:

- Oversize vanity and/or base cabinets

- Shallow wall cabinets

- Medicine cabinet

- Recessed niches

- Freestanding furnishings

- Open shelving

- Hooks and bars

Left: Here's some serious storage! Towering floor cabinets are housed behind warm-stained panel doors, setting a style that complements the equally roomy vanity beyond.

The classic bathroom vanity measures about 32 inches high (including countertop) by 21 inches deep and about 30 inches wide. But bath cabinets are growing—new offerings may be 36 inches (or more) high by 24 inches deep and 48 inches wide. You can make longer cabinet runs by joining pieces together, then bridging them with a single countertop. To make things higher, build up the base or the countertop. If a small space dictates that the vanity must be shallow, pop it out just at the sink, find a smaller sink, or buy a Euro-style fixture that cantilevers off the counter edge (see page 43).

Vanities and other cabinets can house a growing inventory of racks, bins, pullouts, drawer inserts, and lazy Susans available today—making finite storage space ever more efficient.

What if you've fallen in love with a stylish pedestal sink? You'll need to scramble to replace that lost vanity storage. Look to the walls, add tall towers, or carve out recessed niches.

Or do you prefer the "unfitted" look? Individual furnishings can bring a funky, freestanding style to the bath. Choose from new or antique chests, drawers, and armoires, or give new life to a flea-market find.

Many bathroom items are candidates for open storage. Why not display colorful towels, perfume bottles, or stacks of soap on open shelves?

PLAY IT *Safe*

Start your bathroom safety campaign by selecting nonslip fixtures and surface materials. Anchor carpeting, and buy rugs or bath mats that have nonskid backing. Choose tempered glass, plastic, or other shatterproof materials for construction and accessories. Avoid mounting objects such as towel bars with sharp corners at eye level, and plan to clip or round countertop edges.

Install L-shaped or horizontal grab bars, each capable of supporting 300 pounds, in tub and shower areas. Installation must be done properly; plywood reinforcing and bracing between wall studs may be required.

If children live in or visit your house, plan to store medicines and household cleaners in cabinets that have safety latches or locks. Make sure that you can access the bathroom from outside in case of an emergency.

Be sure electrical receptacles are protected by ground fault circuit interrupters (GFCIs), which cut off power immediately if current begins leaking anywhere along the circuit. Outlets should be out of reach from the shower or bathtub. Keep portable heaters out of the bathroom. Install sufficient lighting, including a night-light.

To avoid scalding, lower the setting on your water heater to 120 degrees, install a temperature-limiting mixing valve, or use a pressure-balanced valve to prevent sudden temperature spikes.

About 25 percent of all home accidents occur in the bathroom. Through preventive planning, however, you can greatly reduce the risk of injury in your own bathroom.

GROUND FAULT CIRCUIT INTERRUPTER

Lighting *Guidelines*

GOOD LIGHTING SETS OFF a beautifully decorated bath and ensures a safe and cheery space. Multiple light sources and multiple controls allow you to alternate between morning efficiency and night-time serenity. Start by bringing in natural light through windows and skylights (see pages 56–65), then augment it with a multilayered fixture scheme and multiple switches or dimmers.

Four types of light

Designers separate lighting into four categories: task, ambient, accent, and decorative. You can do the same thing.

Task lighting illuminates a particular area where a visual activity—such as shaving or applying makeup—takes place. Ambient or general lighting fills in the undefined areas of a room with a soft level of light—enough, say, for a relaxing soak in a whirlpool tub. Accent lighting is used to highlight architectural features or attractive prints, to set a mood, or to provide drama. Decorative lighting calls attention to itself—the fixture's the thing, not the light it produces.

Plan first for efficient, flattering task light; then add ambient light to fill in shadows. Stylish master baths and powder rooms present opportunities for both accent and decorative lighting touches.

Left: Incandescent tubes flank twin pedestal sinks, providing even, shadowless grooming light.

A COLOR THERMOMETER

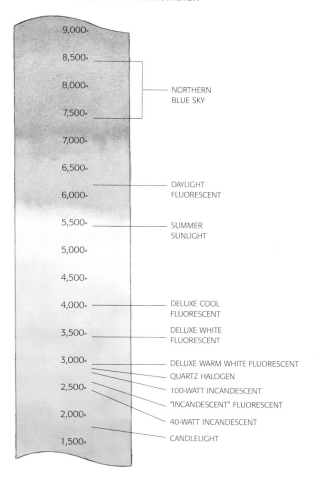

- 9,000°
- 8,500°
- 8,000° — NORTHERN BLUE SKY
- 7,500°
- 7,000°
- 6,500°
- 6,000° — DAYLIGHT FLUORESCENT
- 5,500° — SUMMER SUNLIGHT
- 5,000°
- 4,500°
- 4,000° — DELUXE COOL FLUORESCENT
- 3,500° — DELUXE WHITE FLUORESCENT
- 3,000° — DELUXE WARM WHITE FLUORESCENT
- — QUARTZ HALOGEN
- 2,500° — 100-WATT INCANDESCENT
- — "INCANDESCENT" FLUORESCENT
- 2,000° — 40-WATT INCANDESCENT
- 1,500° — CANDLELIGHT

Above: Classic wall sconces at eye level frame an arched mirror above a pedestal sink.

The color of light

Different light bulbs emit different colors of light, warm to cool. These varying color "temperatures" produce different moods and affect the rendering of nearby room colors.

The old standbys, incandescent A-bulbs, hover near 2,900 degrees Kelvin on the color temperature scale, emitting a warm, familiar light. Fluorescent manufacturers have now developed tubes and bulbs in a wide spectrum of colors, from very warm (about 2,700°K) to very cool (about 6,300°K), though these still won't "read" as warm as A-bulbs. Bright, white halogen sources are the most like daylight; they are excellent for task lighting, pinpoint accenting, and other dramatic accents.

Which fixtures are best?

Generally speaking, "small" and "discreet" are watchwords in bathroom lighting; consequently, recessed downlights are especially popular.

To avoid shadows, place mirror lights at the sides rather than only above the mirror. Wall sconces flanking the mirror provide light and also offer the chance to make a decorative statement.

In a larger bathroom, a separate fixture to light the shower or bath area—or any other distinct part of a compartmentalized room—and perhaps another for reading may be appreciated.

And just for fun, why not consider decorative strip or rope lights in a toe-space area, or even a zoomy neon squiggle? These accents can add a wash of ambient light and also serve as safe, pleasant night-lights.

Heating
and Venting

SOME ELEMENTS OF YOUR BATHROOM'S CLIMATE—
steam, excess heat, early morning chill—can be annoying and
unpleasant. When you remodel, consider adding an efficient exhaust
fan to freshen the air and draw out mold-producing moisture and a
heater to warm you on cool days. Installing such climate controllers
may be simple, and they could make a big difference.

Left: A heated brass towel bar delivers warmth
and charm via old-fashioned hydronics.

Heating it up

Nothing spoils the soothing effects of a long,
hot soak or shower faster than stepping out
into a cool room—even one that's the same
temperature as the rest of the house. For
comfort, aim to raise the bathroom temperature about 5 to 10 degrees above the level
throughout the rest of the house. A small
auxiliary heater in the wall or ceiling may be
all you need to stay cozy while toweling off.

Because electric heaters are easy to install
and clean to operate, they're the most familiar
choice. In addition to the standard wall- and
ceiling-mounted units, you'll find heaters
combined with exhaust fans, lights, or both.
Add a timer and you can wake up to a toasty
bathing space. Many units require a dedicated
120- or 240-volt circuit, so shop carefully.

Gas heaters that can be recessed into a wall
between two studs are available in a variety
of styles and sizes. Regardless of how they

Right: Radiant-heat coils are laid below thin-set adhesive, then covered with porcelain floor tiles. The coils come in both hydronic and electric versions.

heat, all gas models require a gas supply line and must be vented to the outside.

Another heat source has reappeared on the bathroom scene: hot water. The original idea was to warm and dry bath towels, but now these hydronic units—either wall- or floor-mounted—are being billed as room-warming "radiators" as well. As for towel warmers, you'll find sleek electric versions (see page 89) in addition to water-powered ones.

If you're planning a remodel that will have stone or ceramic tile flooring, consider adding cozy radiant-heat coils below the floor.

Ventilating the bathroom

You can buy fans to mount in the wall or in the ceiling. Some models also include a light, heat lamps, or both.

It's important that your exhaust fan have adequate capacity. The Home Ventilating Institute (HVI) recommends that the fan be capable of exchanging the air at least eight times each hour. To determine the required fan

PROGRAMMABLE TIMER SWITCH

capacity in cubic feet per minute (CFM) for a bathroom with an 8-foot ceiling, multiply the room's length and width in feet by 1.1. For example, if your bathroom is 6 by 9 feet, you would calculate the required fan capacity this way:

CEILING FAN

$$6 \times 9 \times 1.1 = 59.4 \text{ CFM}$$

Rounding off, you would need a fan capacity of at least 60 CFM. If your fan must exhaust through a long duct or several elbows, you'll need greater capacity to overcome the increased resistance. Follow the manufacturer's recommendations.

Most fans have a noise rating measured in "sones." The lower the number (such as 1.5), the quieter the fan.

Ideally, your fan should be mounted as close as possible to the shower or tub. It should also be as far as possible from the source of re-placement air (the door, for instance).

Remodeling
Realities

IF ALL IT WILL TAKE TO UPDATE YOUR BATHROOM is a new vanity, a faucet, and some wallpaper, you probably won't need to find out just what lurks behind those walls. But if you're shifting or adding fixtures, installing a vent fan, or removing a wall, you'll have to bone up on some basic remodeling realities. These next pages offer an overview of bathroom systems.

Structural changes

If you're planning to open up a space, add a skylight, or recess a shower or tub unit into the floor, your remodel may require structural modifications.

Your bathroom's framework likely conforms to the pattern of the "typical house" shown on the facing page. Starting at the base of the drawing, you'll notice these framing members: a series of horizontal, evenly spaced floor joists and a subfloor (usually plywood sheets) laid atop the joists. The walls are formed by vertical studs that run between a horizontal sole plate and a parallel top plate. The primary wall coverings are fastened directly to the studs. If there's another story above, another layer of joists rests on the walls. A one-story house will have either an "open-beamed" ceiling or a "finished" ceiling, with the ceiling materials attached directly to the joists.

Left: An attic remodel tucks a pedestal tub and a window into the narrow gable wall below roof rafters; a storage niche at right makes use of hollow wall space.

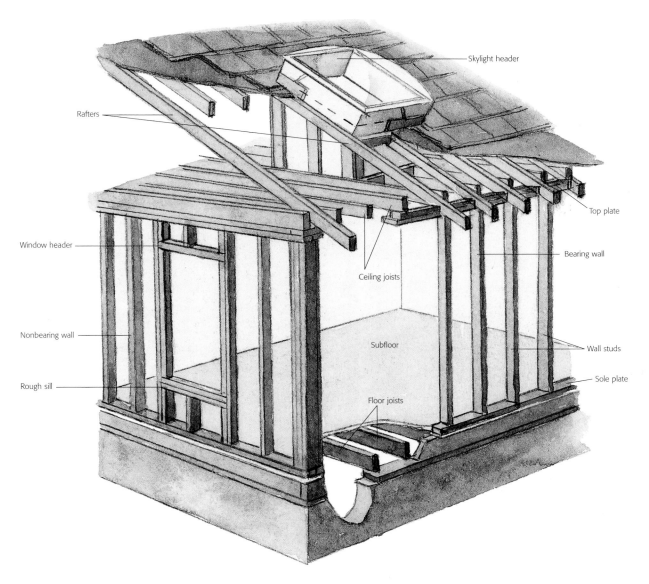

Rafters

Skylight header

Window header

Ceiling joists

Top plate

Bearing wall

Nonbearing wall

Subfloor

Wall studs

Rough sill

Sole plate

Floor joists

Walls are either bearing (supporting the weight of ceiling joists, rafters, and/or second-story walls) or nonbearing. If you're removing all or part of a bearing wall, you must bridge the gap with a sturdy beam and posts. Nonbearing (partition) walls can usually be removed without too much trouble—unless pipes or wires run through them.

Doors and windows require special framing, as shown; the size of the header depends on the width of the opening and your local building codes. Skylights require similar cuts through ceiling joists and/or rafters.

A standard doorway may not be large enough to accommodate a new tub or whirlpool. If you're remodeling,

make sure you can get such a fixture into the room!

Hardwood, ceramic, or stone floors require very stiff underlayment. You may need to beef up the floor joists and/or add additional plywood or cement backerboard on top. For a large new tub, you may also need to supply strong floor framing.

Plumbing restrictions

Your plumbing system is composed of two parts: a water-supply system, which brings water to the house and distributes it, and a drain-waste-vent (DWV) system, which removes waste and water.

Every house has a main soil stack. Below the level of the fixtures, it's the primary drainpipe. At its upper end, which protrudes through the roof, the stack becomes a vent. To minimize costs and keep the work simple, arrange a fixture or a group of fixtures as close as possible to existing pipes.

A proposed fixture within a few feet of the main stack usually can be vented directly by the stack. Sometimes a fixture located far from the main stack requires its own branch drain and a secondary vent stack—a big job. Be sure to check your local plumbing codes for exact requirements.

It's generally an easy matter—at least conceptually—to extend water-supply pipes to a new sink or tub. But if you're working on a concrete slab foundation, you'll need to drill through the slab or bring the pipes through the wall from another point above floor level.

SHUTOFF VALVE

PLUMBING SYSTEMS

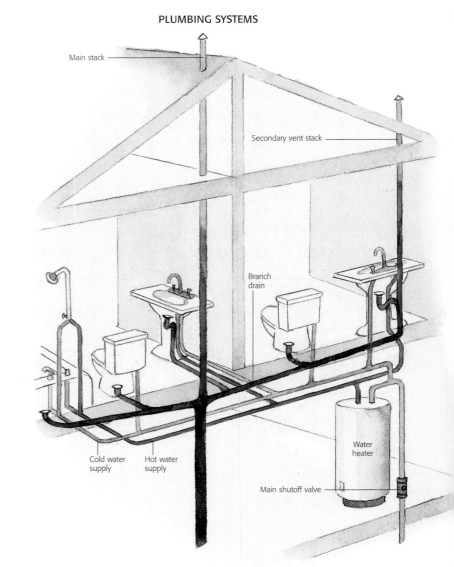

Main stack

Secondary vent stack

Branch drain

Water heater

Cold water supply

Hot water supply

Main shutoff valve

COPPER SUPPLY PIPE

DWV FITTINGS

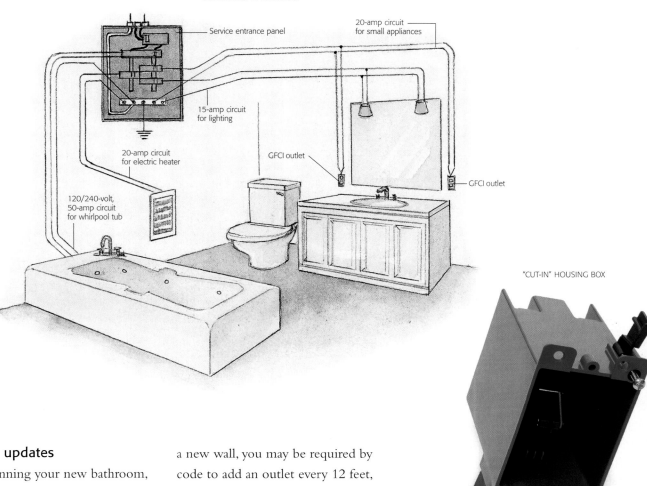

Service entrance panel

20-amp circuit
for small appliances

15-amp circuit
for lighting

20-amp circuit
for electric heater

GFCI outlet

GFCI outlet

120/240-volt,
50-amp circuit
for whirlpool tub

"CUT-IN" HOUSING BOX

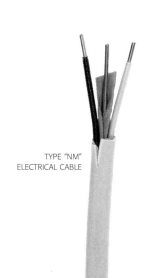

TYPE "NM"
ELECTRICAL CABLE

Electrical updates

When planning your new bathroom, take a good look at the existing electrical system. Most houses today have both 120-volt and 240-volt capabilities. But older homes with two-wire (120 volts only) service of less than 100 amps might not be able to supply the electricity needed to operate a new whirlpool tub, a sauna, a steam generator, or an electric heater. You may need to upgrade your electrical system.

The National Electrical Code (NEC) requires that all bathroom receptacles be protected by ground fault circuit interrupters (GFCIs). If you're adding a new wall, you may be required by code to add an outlet every 12 feet, or one per wall. Codes may strictly dictate the placement of outlets, appliance switches, and even light fixtures in wet areas.

While it's possible to locate electrical wiring inside surface-mounted conduit, it's usually far preferable to enclose all wires within the walls. Before completing your plan, try to track down any plumbing pipes, heating ducts, or electrical wires already concealed there; sleuth from open areas (the basement, the attic, an unfinished garage) to identify spots where such utilities enter the walls.

Putting It *All Together*

ONCE YOU'VE WORKED OUT an efficient layout, decided on storage requirements, and planned color and design schemes, it's time to draw up a revised floor plan. Be sure to think about light fixtures and electrical switches and receptacles. And don't forget finishing touches such as doorknobs and drawer pulls, towel bars and moldings, curtains and blinds—details that can really pull a design together.

The final plan

Create a new floor plan, or working drawing, the same way you made your original scale plan (see page 94). On the new plan, include existing features you want to preserve and all the changes you want to make. If you prefer, you can hire a designer, drafter, or contractor to draw the final plan for you. Elevation (head-on) sketches usually aren't required, but they'll prove helpful in planning the work.

For complicated projects, your local building department may require detailed drawings of structural, plumbing, and wiring changes. You may also need to show areas adjacent to the bathroom so officials can determine how the project will affect the rest of your house. To discover just which codes may affect your project and whether a permit is required, check with your city or county building department.

Left: Here's where fixtures and surface materials take their final form. A steel window, stone tiles, and warm wood complete this platform tub.

NEED *Help?*

To help you decipher what kind of help you may need, the following listing covers various professionals in bathroom design and construction.

■ **Architects** are state-licensed professionals with degrees in architecture. Trained to create structurally sound and functional designs, they know construction materials, can negotiate bids from contractors, and can supervise the actual work. Many are members of the American Institute of Architects (AIA). If structural calculations must be made, architects can make them; other professionals need state-licensed engineers to design structures and sign working drawings. Some architects may be less familiar than other specialists with the latest in bathroom design and materials.

■ **Bathroom designers** know the hottest trends in fixtures and furnishings, but they may lack the structural knowledge of the architect and the aesthetic skill of a good interior designer. If you decide to work with a bathroom designer, look for a member of the National Kitchen & Bath Association (NKBA) or a Certified Bathroom Designer (CBD), a specialist certified by the NKBA. These associations have established codes and sponsor continuing programs about the latest building materials and techniques.

■ **Interior designers** specialize in the decorating and furnishing of rooms and can offer innovative ideas and advice. Through their contacts, a homeowner has access to materials and products not available at the retail level. Even

if you're working with an architect or a bathroom designer, you may wish to call on an interior designer for finishing touches. Some offer complete remodeling services. Many belong to the American Society of Interior Designers (ASID), a professional organization.

■ **Retail specialists** include showroom personnel, building-center staff, and other professionals. If your bathroom requires only a minor face-lift, this kind of help may be all you need. If you're tackling a larger job, check the specialist's qualifications carefully. Typically, you provide a rough floor plan and fill out a questionnaire; the retailer provides a finished plan and/or materials list—if you buy its goods.

■ **General contractors** specialize in construction, although some have design skills as well. General contractors may do all the work themselves or assume responsibility for hiring qualified subcontractors, ordering construction materials, and seeing that the job is completed according to contract. Contractors can secure building permits and arrange for inspections as work progresses.

Can you do it yourself?

Be realistic when assessing your do-it-yourself abilities. The skill level required for a bathroom remodel depends on what improvements you are making. Surface treatments—such as painting, wallpapering, or simply replacing light fixtures—can be accomplished by any homeowner who has a little do-it-yourself experience. Some projects may require specialized tools, usually available from any home improvement center.

Complex remodeling tasks—such as moving load-bearing walls, running new drain and vent pipes, or wiring new electrical circuits—often are best handled by professionals. Smaller jobs within these areas, though, are within the skills of an experienced homeowner.

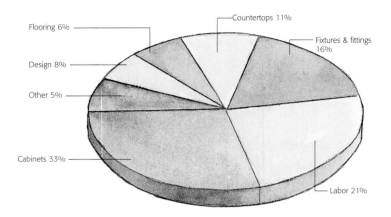

PIECES OF THE BUDGET PIE

Flooring 6%
Design 8%
Other 5%
Cabinets 33%
Countertops 11%
Fixtures & fittings 16%
Labor 21%

Left: A few special tiles in a larger field of inexpensive, machined tiles add a custom touch—without breaking the budget.

Dollars and cents

OK, so how much will your new bathroom cost? According to the National Kitchen & Bath Association, the average figure is around $10,000. This is, of course, only the sketchiest of estimates. You may simply need to replace a countertop, add light fixtures, or exchange a worn-out bathtub to achieve a satisfying change. On the other hand, extensive structural changes coupled with ultra-high-end materials and fixtures can easily add up.

As shown above, labor typically eats up 21 percent of the pie; cabinets come in at around 33 percent;

and, on the average, fixtures and fittings represent another 16 percent. Structural, plumbing, and electrical changes all affect the final figure significantly.

How do you keep the budget in check? For starters, identify whether you're looking at a simple face-lift, a more extensive replacement, or a major structural remodel. Fixture, fitting, and material prices vary greatly. Obtain ballpark figures in different categories, mull them over, and then present your architect, designer, or retailer with a range of options and a bottom line with which you are comfortable. Of course, you can save a substantial piece of the pie by providing labor yourself—but be sure you're up to the task!

If you use a design professional, expect to be charged either a flat fee or a percentage (usually 10 to 15 percent) of the total cost of goods purchased. General contractors include their fees in their bids.

BUILDER/PLANNER
Checklist

This list can help you plan the sequence of tasks involved in dismantling your old bathroom and installing the new one. Depending on the size of your job and the materials you select, you may need to alter the suggested order somewhat. Manufacturers' instructions offer additional guidelines.

Above: A builder's basic tool kit includes safety goggles or glasses, gloves, hearing protection, and a dust mask or respirator.

Removal sequence

1. Accessories, decorative elements
2. Furniture, if any
3. Contents of cabinets, closets, shelves
4. Plumbing hookups
5. Fixtures
6. Vanity countertops
7. Vanity cabinets, recessed cabinets, shelves
8. Flooring
9. Light fixtures
10. Wall and ceiling coverings

Installation sequence

1. Structural changes: walls, doors, windows, skylights
2. Rough plumbing changes
3. Electrical wiring
4. Bathtub, shower
5. Wall and ceiling coverings
6. Light fixtures
7. Cabinets, countertops
8. Toilet, bidet, sink
9. Finish flooring
10. Decorative elements

CORDLESS DRIVER/DRILL

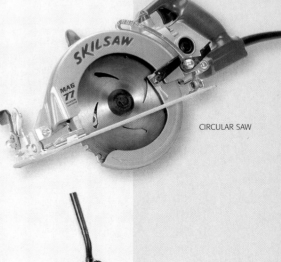

CIRCULAR SAW

SOLDERING TORCH

Color
Palettes

CREATING A COLOR SCHEME for your bathroom can be
daunting. How can you be certain that the colors you like will work
together in a room? Here are "real-life" color combinations that
homeowners and designers chose for bathrooms shown in this book.
The page number under each palette refers to the photo showcasing
it. You can use these palettes as is or alter them to fit your own plan.

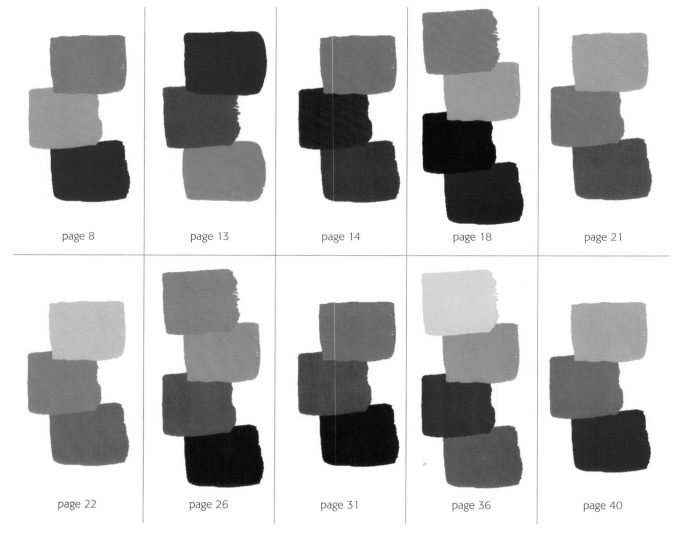

| page 8 | page 13 | page 14 | page 18 | page 21 |

| page 22 | page 26 | page 31 | page 36 | page 40 |

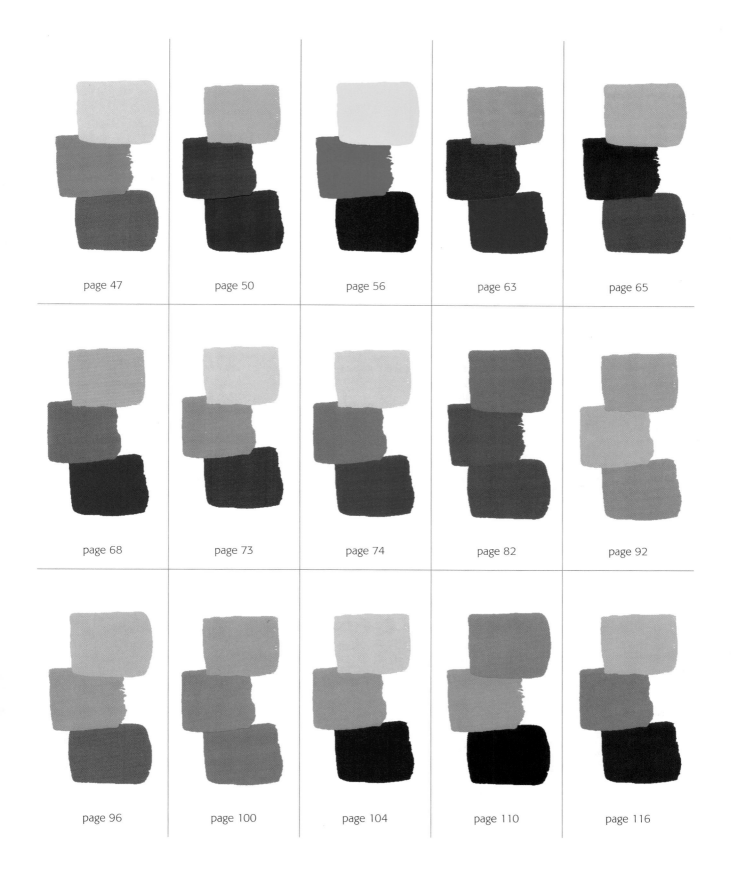

page 47

page 50

page 56

page 63

page 65

page 68

page 73

page 74

page 82

page 92

page 96

page 100

page 104

page 110

page 116

Design and Photography Credits

DESIGN

Front Matter

2 left William Gottlieb and Markie Nelson **2 right** Hutker Architects **3 bottom right** Heidi Richardson/Richardson Architects **5** Paul Vincent Wiseman

Ideas and Inspiration

6 Hutker Architects **7 right** Perry Dean Rogers + Partners/Steven Foote Architect **8** Architect: Halperin & Christ; Interior design: Sharon Low; Contractor: Rempe Construction **9 top** Jennifer Madden and Jeff Reed **9 bottom** Steve Howard **10** Walter Metez Architects **11 top left** Architect: Joel Pathman **11 center right** Deena Rauen/D Studio **11 bottom left** John Knudson (Knudson Gloss Architects/Planners) **12 top left and right** Interior design: Tracey Kessler/t.k.i.d.; Contractor: Philip Combs/Universe Construction **12 bottom left** Stylist: James Day, NYC **13** Architect: Halperin & Christ **14** Architect: Halperin & Christ; Builder: Roc Builders **15 top left** Sasha Emerson Levin **15 middle right** Architect: Halperin & Christ; Interior design: Sharon Low **15 bottom left** Jerome Buttrick/Buttrick Wong Architects **17 middle left and bottom right** Architects: Jeffrey L. Day/Min-Day and Marc Toma and Lisa K. Trujillo/BurksToma; Interior design: Marie Fisher and Alissa Lillie/Marie Fisher Interior Design **17 top right** Melanie Born **18** Architect: John Hermannson; Design and installation: Toni Deser and Paul Rodman **19 bottom right** Jerome Buttrick/Buttrick Wong Architects **20 top left and bottom left** Philip J. Meyer Ltd. **21** Vasken Guiragossian **22–23 all** Regan Bice Architects **24** Hutker Architects **25 top** Remick Associates Architects-Builders, Inc. **25 bottom** Malibu Ceramic Works **26** Architect: John Peterson/Peterson Architects; Interior design: Judy Hallden Design; Lighting design: Becca Foster Lighting Design **27 top left** Paulett Taggart Architects **27 middle right** Archeo Architects **27 bottom left** Charles Debbas; Contractor: Kevin Reimer/The

Builder Group **29 top right** Remick Associates Architects-Builders, Inc.; Tile: Stonelight Tile Company **29 center left** Architect: Halperin & Christ; Interior design: Gill Hayward; Contractor: Jeff Bayles **29 bottom right** Architect: Jonathan Pearlman/Elevation Architects; Interior design: LouAnn Bauer ASID/Bauer Interior Design **30 top left** Builder: McMillen Inc. **31 top** Fu-Tung Cheng/Cheng Design **31 bottom left** Ashley Jenkins/Ashley Roi Jenkins Designs **32 bottom left** Masland Carpets & Rugs **32 bottom right** Melinda D. Douros **33 top right** Formica Corporation **33 bottom left** Heidi M. Emmett **33 bottom right** San Francisco Design Center "idea house" **35 top right and bottom right** Susan Sargent Designs **36** Architect: Halperin & Christ; Contractor: Jeff Bayles **37 top right** Architect and builder: Halperin & Christ **37 center left** Ryan Gainey **37 bottom right** Steven Kahner, Architect **38 bottom right** Heidi M. Emmett **39 bottom right** Dominic Mercadante, Architect **40** Architect: John Hermannson; Design and installation: Toni Deser and Paul Rodman **41 top** Legler + Lievre **41 bottom** Fred Eric **42 top left** Duffy Design Group **42 bottom left** Architect: Frank Hennessy; Interior design: Miller/Stein Interior Design **42 top right** Waterworks **43 bottom left** Lamperti Associates/Schlanser Design **44 bottom left** Architect: Halperin & Christ; Interior design: Gill Hayward; Contractor: Jeff Bayles **44 bottom center** Kitchens & More **44 bottom right** Bath and Beyond **45 top left** Architect: Halperin & Christ; Interior design: Sharon Low; Contractor: Cam Fraser **45 top center and lower right** Kohler **46 top** Fu-Tung Cheng/Cheng Design **46 bottom** Morimoto Architects **47** J. Reed Robbins **48 top** Crane Plumbing **48 bottom center** Kohler **49 top** SkB Architects **49 bottom** Remick Associates Architects-Builders, Inc. **50 top** Elliott, Elliott, Norelius Architecture **50 bottom** Architect: Tim Andreas **51 top** Architect: Bernie Baker **51 bottom left** Tile artisan: Marlo Bartels Studio of Laguna Beach **51 bottom right** Joe Sturges

52 top Crane Plumbing **52 top center left** Delta **52 bottom left** Kohler **53 top right** Architect: Halperin & Christ; Interior design: Sharon Low; Contractor: Rempe Construction **53 bottom** Bath and Beyond **54 top center left** Bath and Beyond **54 bottom left** Architect: Michael Harris Architecture; Lighting design: Becca Foster Lighting Design; Contractor: Peter Harris; Cabinets: Michael Dotter/Sun Woodworks **55 top right** Design: Cia Foreman; Contractor: Ron Middel **55 bottom left and center** Bath and Beyond **55 bottom right** Kohler **56** Mercedes Corbell Design + Architecture **57 bottom** Bohlin **58** Lighting design: Linda Ferry; Architect: Charles Rose; Glass artist: Masaoka Glass Design **60 center left** David Vandervort **60 top right** Architect: Scott Johnson **61** Remick Associates Architects-Builders, Inc. **62 both** Lighting design: Melinda Morrison Lighting Design; Architects: Byron Kuth, Liz Ranieri, Doug Thornley (Kuth/Ranieri Architects) **63** Architect: Backen, Arragoni & Ross **64 top left** Kuth/Ranieri Architects **65** Lighting design: Randall Whitehead Lighting Inc.; Architect: Erikson Zebroski Design Group **67 top** Christine E. Barnes **67 bottom** Kohler **68** SkB Architects **69 top** Kerry Joyce **69 bottom** Katherine North/Northbrook Design **70 top left** Melinda Douros and D. Kimberly Smith/Deer Creek Design **70 bottom left** Kit Parmentier/Allison Rose **71 top** Designs Northwest Architects and Garrett Kuhlman/H2K Design **71 bottom** Ron Sutton/Sutton Suzuki Architects **72 top left** Architect: Dave Maynard; Design: Jackson Butler **72 bottom left** Interior design: Ruth Soforenko Associates; Architect: Heidi Hansen; Contractor: Bob Rosenberg **72 center right** Pottery Barn **73** Architect: Halperin & Christ; Contractor: Jeff Bayles **74** Mark Rios **75 center right** Decorative painter: Erik Seniska **75 bottom left** Architect: Sally Weston **76 top left** Kathy Farley/Artdecor **76 top right** Melinda Douros and D. Kimberly Smith/Deer Creek Design

Index

Numbers in **boldface** type refer to photographs or drawings.

CORE COLLECTION 2005